Photograph by Joel Gardner

John Gardner
A Bibliographical Profile

By John M. Howell

With an Afterword by John Gardner

Southern Illinois University Press
Carbondale and Edwardsville
Feffer & Simons, Inc.
London and Amsterdam

012
C-227h

Copyright © 1980 by Southern Illinois University Press
All rights reserved
Printed in the United States of America
Designed by Richard Neal

Library of Congress Cataloging in Publication Data

Howell, John Michael, 1933–.
  John Gardner, a bibliographical profile.

  Includes bibliographical references.
  1. Gardner, John Champlin, 1933–   —Bibliography.
I. Title.
Z8324.17.H68   [PS3557.A712]   016.813'5'4   79-22167
ISBN 0-8093-0935-1

For Sue and Evan

Contents

List of Illustrations

Preface

John Gardner is, as reviewers have observed, a "philosophical novelist." Despite this bearish label, three of his novels to date have been best sellers, and one, *October Light*, received the National Book Critics Circle Award for Fiction in 1976. Gardner is also called a "fabulator." But though he may, as he says, "put on a circus show," or "throw his voice," or "play magic games" with his characters, his vision is essentially tragic. He celebrates the same enduring truths that Homer, Tolstoy, and Faulkner celebrated in the past. His aim, he says, is to write a "moral fiction," a fiction which stands in creative opposition to the "monstrousness" of Sartrean existentialism and affirms the redeeming power of the imagination.

At last count Gardner had published over thirty books, pamphlets, and broadsides; over one hundred stories, poems, articles, essays, and reviews; and over one hundred interviews. Yet only a few short, enumerative bibliographies, including my own, have been published.* This full-length bibliography is an attempt to remedy this fact and lay the necessary groundwork for scholars and critics who wish to explore the genesis of Gardner's thought, art, and reputation.

This bibliography provides: 1) a biographical outline of Gardner's career; 2) a collation of the first American edition, with photographic reproductions of its title and copyright pages; 3) printing histories of the first American and British editions; 4) printing histories of all subsequent editions in boards and wrappers; 5) citations of all verifiable foreign editions; 6) annotated checklists of all forthcoming and projected works; 7) annotated checklists of all fiction, poetry, articles, essays, reviews, and letters; 8) an annotated checklist of interviews and speeches; 9) a miscellaneous checklist of Gardner's manuscripts and contributions to other media; 10) a secondary checklist of articles and essays; 11) a secondary checklist of reviews. In addition, the reader will find photographic reproductions of significant typescript pages, memorabilia, and dust jackets.

Section A of this bibliography records editions and printings of all separate publications. It identifies editions by arabic numerals: "1" is the first edition, "2" the second edition, and so on. It identifies printings by lowercase roman letters: "a" is the first printing, "b" the second printing. Since I have not always been able to verify copyright claims of simultane-

*Anon., *John Gardner: First Decade: Collected Works: 1962–1973* (Southfield, Mich.: n.p., October 1973); Gary M. Lepper, "John Gardner," *A Bibliographical Introduction to Seventy-Five Modern American Authors* (Berkeley: Serendipity Books, 1976), pp. 209–11; David A. Dillon, "John C. Gardner: A Bibliography," *Bulletin of Bibliography*, 34 (April–June 1977), 86–89, 104; and John M. Howell, "John Gardner 1933–," *First Printings of American Authors*, Vol. III (Detroit: Gale Research Co., 1978, pp. 117–23).

ous publication in Canada, I have excluded Canadian issues, as opposed to printings, from the bibliography.

All printings I have not personally seen have been verified through correspondence with the publishers, as indicated by ''source'' notes to the entry. With the exception of *Nickel Mountain, The Motorcycle Riders,* and *The Crow,* all the title pages in Section A were printed in black type on white paper. The abbreviations used indicate the following: *CLC, Contemporary Literary Criticism;* DLC, Library of Congress; JG, John Gardner's private collection; JH, John Howell's private collection; SIU-C, Southern Illinois University at Carbondale (Morris Library).

John M. Howell
Carbondale, Illinois
August 1979

Acknowledgments

I have been a close observer of John Gardner's prodigious output since September 1965, when he joined the faculty of the English department at Southern Illinois University in Carbondale. But I did not find the courage to begin this bibliography until August 1976, after spending a few days with him at his home in Bennington, Vermont. In venturing forth, I had, in addition to the cooperation of the author, the moral as well as technical support of two excellent bibliographers: Alan M. Cohn and David V. Koch, both of the Morris Library at Southern Illinois University. I welcome this opportunity of formally thanking them for their generous assistance.

I also wish to thank at least a few others among my more than one hundred collaborators. The following were particularly helpful: Matthew J. Bruccoli and Joseph Katz, of the University of South Carolina; Robert Gottlieb, Lee Goerner, Carole Frankel, and William Luckey, of Alfred A. Knopf, Inc.; Anne Borchardt, of Georges Borchardt, Inc.; Cameron Northouse, of New London Press; Herb Yellin, of Lord John Press; Jean Palmer, of Random House, Inc.; Fred Dodnick, of Bantam Books, Inc.; Heinz Roeber, of G. K. Hall, Inc.; Fabio Coen, of Pantheon Books, Inc.; William E. Reinhardt, of Book-of-the Month Club, Inc.; Lauri Goldman, of The Literary Guild, Inc.; William Ashworth, of Harper and Row, Inc.; Irwin S. Kern, of the United States Information Service; Sander Zulauf, of the *Index of American Periodical Verse;* Tom Maschler, Graham C. Greene, and Jeanne Sheriff, of Jonathan Cape, Ltd.; and Philip Tammer, of André Deutsch, Publishers.

Of those scholars and librarians who assisted me, I am particularly grateful to Sandy Eckenbrecht, Lloyd Worley, Kathleen Eads, and Hensley Woodbridge, Southern Illinois University at Carbondale; Karl Kabelac, University of Rochester; William A. Jones, Chico State University; Ruth Kern, George Mason University; William Heyen and John Maier, State University of New York College at Brockport; Holly Hall, Washington University; N. W. Stoddard, *St. Louis Post-Dispatch;* Rex Shaeffer, *Rochester Times-Union* and *Democrat & Chronicle;* Marilyn Annan, *New York Times;* Dorothy S. Belniak, *Bennington Banner;* John W. Garland, University of Detroit; Hal Hall, Texas A & M University; Virginia B. Harris, Oberlin College; Norma Hovden, University of Minnesota; Kathleen Owens, DePauw University; Thomas Quinlan, University of Iowa; Barbara O. Hicks, Southern Methodist University; Michelle Ann Kapecky, *Detroit Free Press;* Carolyn Weasner, Hiram College; William Hifner, *Washington Post;* Thomas Glastros, Indiana University; Elizabeth H. Schumann, Brown University; and Robert Buckeye, Middlebury College.

Of those friends and relatives of Gardner who assisted me, I wish to

thank especially: Joan Patterson Gardner, Priscilla Jones Gardner, Joe
Baber, Helen Vergette, Cal and Brent Riley, Harry and Beatrice Moore, Bob
Griffin, Sidney Moss, Herb Fink, and Tom Walsh.

Finally, I wish to thank the three divisions of Southern Illinois University
at Carbondale that made this bibliography possible. I thank the Graduate
Office of Research and Projects, which supported me with funds for
research assistance and photography. I thank the Department of English,
whose chairpersons—Ted Boyle, Bob Partlow, and Bill Simeone—
supported me with released time from teaching and supplied me with the
secretarial assistance of Pauline Duke and her excellent staff. And I thank
the Southern Illinois University Press, particularly Teresa White, who did
the final editing of the manuscript; and the late Vernon Sternberg, who
gave me the initial impetus and encouragement.

Chronology

1933–1946

John Champlin Gardner, Jr., was born 21 July 1933 in Batavia, New York, to John Champlin and Priscilla Jones Gardner. Nicknamed "Bud"—Welsh "Budd," the poet—he is the eldest of four children raised on a dairy farm outside of Batavia. Though his environment was rural, his literary interests were stimulated by his father, a lay preacher and public reader; and by his mother, an English teacher in the local schools. He began writing "novels" and poems at eleven. A strong interest in the Boy Scouts, which held their meetings at the First Presbyterian Church in Batavia, eventually led to his becoming an Eagle Scout and "Mayor of Batavia" for a day. A crucial incident in his life was the death, on 4 April 1945, of his brother Gilbert, run over by a cultipacker that Gardner was pulling with a tractor.

1946–1951

While attending high school at Alexander Central School, he drew a cartoon of an elephant in Mary Greco's art class and, at her encouragement, sent the cartoon to *Seventeen Magazine*, which published it in July 1948. It was, apparently, his first "professional" publication. During this period, and later, after transferring to Batavia High School, he took lessons on the French horn at the Eastman School of Music's Preparatory School in nearby Rochester. Upon graduation from high school, in 1951, he entered DePauw University, where he planned to major in chemistry.

1951–1955

At DePauw his literary interests began to develop. He published a story in the campus magazine and wrote the book and lyrics for a musical comedy entitled *The Caucus Race*, which won the Monon script competition and was produced 11–13 February 1954 as the "1954 Monon Revue." By the time of its production, however, Gardner had transferred to Washington University in St. Louis, a move inspired by his marriage to Joan Louise Patterson on 6 June 1953. During the two years he attended Washington University, Gardner came under the influence of Jarvis Thurston, editor of *Perspective* and, Gardner claims, one of the two finest teachers he ever encountered (the other was John C. McGalliard of the University of Iowa). Under Thurston he began early versions of what would later evolve into chapters of *Nickel Mountain*. In his senior year (1954–55) he was elected to Phi Beta Kappa and won a Woodrow Wilson Fellowship. His interests were by now clearly literary and philosophical.

1955–1958

Gardner used his fellowship to support his enrollment in the creative writing program at the University of Iowa. Unhappy with the writing workshops, he chose instead to work individually with Calvin Kentfield, Robert O. Bowen, Vance Bourjaily, and Marguerite Young. Though he "wrote no poetry" during this period, his most important friends and critics were Donald Finkel, Constance Urdang, and William Dickey—all students in the poetry workshop. He was awarded an M.A. degree for a creative thesis entitled "Four Short Stories" ("Darkling Wood," "One Saturday Morning," "Peter Willis, Resting"—a version of an early *Nickel Mountain* element—and "Nickel Mountain"). His interest in scholarship—especially languages—was keener than ever, however, and when he went on for his doctorate he began to work regularly with John C. McGalliard in Anglo-Saxon and Medieval Studies, a key factor in the direction of his art. By the time he took his Ph.D in 1958, he had completed two novels: "The Old Men," which he submitted as his dissertation, and "Sparrows," which, like "The Old Men," remains unpublished.

1958–1962

Upon graduation in 1958 Gardner began a series of short academic appointments. In September 1958, he accepted a lectureship at Oberlin College, where he taught freshman English, world literature, and, as an extra course, creative writing. Fired, he maintains, for leading a three-week faculty strike, he accepted a lectureship, in September 1959, at Chico State College (now the University of California at Chico), where he would remain for three years, and where both his children would be born: his son, Joel (31 December 1959); and his daughter, Lucy (3 January 1962). Hired to teach creative writing and to write a history of the college, he also supervised the publication of the student literary magazine *Selection*. Assisting him was Lennis Dunlap, a colleague in the English department who later collaborated with Gardner in editing Gardner's first book publication, *The Forms of Fiction* (1962). When the administration of the college irritated Gardner by attempting to censor *Selection*, he ended its publication in 1961 and began a professional magazine called *MSS*, which, though it only lasted three numbers (1961, 1962, and 1964), won considerable prestige by publishing such writers as Joyce Carol Oates, William Gass, John Hawkes, Howard Nemerov, George P. Elliott, William Stafford, William Palmer, and W. S. Merwin. In the meantime Gardner had completed *The Resurrection*, a version of *Nickel Mountain*, five "clown plays," including "The Birds" and "The Latest Word from Delphi"; and he had worked on "The Roaring Sheep," an as yet unpublished novel, which he began at Iowa and returned to periodically up through 1969. It was his scholarship, however, that won him an appointment as an assistant professor to teach medieval studies at

San Francisco State College (now the University of California at San Francisco).

1962–1965

At San Francisco State he joined an English faculty that included such writers and critics as Ruby Cohn, William Dickey, Mark Harris, and Wright Morris. Freed from the pressures of reading "creative writing," Gardner completed translations of *The Alliterative Morte Arthure* and *The Complete Works of the Gawain-Poet;* and wrote a thousand-page study of the life and works of Geoffrey Chaucer. In October 1964 New American Library accepted *The Resurrection* and gave Gardner hope that they might also publish *Nickel Mountain.* Encouraged by this response, he began what was to become *The Sunlight Dialogues,* though the opening focused on a monk in a monastery and is barely recognizable as having any relationship to the published work.

1965–1969

The Complete Works of the Gawain-Poet was published 31 August 1965—three weeks before Gardner began his appointment as associate professor of Anglo-Saxon and Medieval Studies at Southern Illinois University in Carbondale. Buying a farm on Boskydell Road, a few miles south of Carbondale, Gardner continued work on *The Sunlight Dialogues.* Alternating between it, "The Roaring Sheep," poetry, and scholarly studies—including an early draft of what he would later call "On Moral Fiction"—Gardner created a textual critic's nightmare. By January 1966 he had dropped the monk from *The Sunlight Dialogues* and focused on Clumly, the police chief, as the protagonist. By the time *The Resurrection* was published on 22 June 1966, *The Sunlight Dialogues* was well under way. By March 1968, he had completed it. And by April 1969, it had been rejected by at least three publishers, including Farrar, Straus, & Giroux; Macmillan; and Houghton Mifflin. In the meantime, after two false starts, Gardner had begun *The Wreckage of Agathon,* which he was calling "The Last Days of the Seer," and which he would complete by August 1969. Directly after completing it, he began *Grendel.*

1970

By April 1970 he had completed *Grendel* and begun, with the assistance of his wife, Joan, *The Smugglers of Lost Souls' Rock*—the novel within the novel of *October Light.* In the summer of 1970, while in York, England, Gardner began *Jason and Medeia,* which he was then calling "Jason: An Epic." By the time *The Wreckage of Agathon* was published on 23 September 1970, Gardner was Distinguished Visiting Professor for the fall semester at the University of Detroit, he had won a Danforth Fellowship, and his agent,

Georges Borchardt, was negotiating the sale of *Grendel* and *The Sunlight Dialogues* to Knopf. Gardner's elation at selling these two novels was tempered, however, by the death of his editor and champion, David Segal, who recognized Gardner's talent when Gardner submitted *The Resurrection* to New American Library, where Segal was employed at the time. When Segal moved to Harper & Row he bought and edited *The Wreckage of Agathon*. When he moved to Knopf he bought *The Sunlight Dialogues* and *Grendel*. After Segal's death Gardner renewed his request, in a letter dated 22 January 1971, that Knopf illustrate his novels. His new editor, Robert Gottlieb, who was later to become president of Knopf, agreed and the illustrated novel for adults was reborn.

1971

Apart from work on scholarly projects, Gardner spent the spring and summer of 1971 writing most of the stories collected in *The King's Indian*, including the title novella, which he was at this time calling "Augusta." By the time *Grendel* was published (17 September), followed by *The Alliterative Morte Arthure* (27 September), Gardner was in London for a sabbatical year, working on, among other things, a film about a psychic professor, written for Telly Savalas (never made), and *Jason and Medeia*.

1972

Gardner had completed a draft of *Jason and Medeia* by early February. At this time he turned again to *Nickel Mountain*, the episodic novel of his apprenticeship. Cutting and revising, he introduced the pastoral metaphor as a unifying device. After, or during, the reworking of *Nickel Mountain*, he began "Somnium Guthlaci," an as yet uncompleted dream poem. The year ended with his winning a grant from the National Endowment for the Arts—and his first popular success as a novelist with the publication of *The Sunlight Dialogues* on 6 December.

1973

Gardner began the year as a visiting professor for the winter quarter at Northwestern University. Winning a Guggenheim Fellowship for 1973–74, he again took a leave from Southern Illinois University. By the time *Jason and Medeia* was published, on 21 June, he had completed his study of the Wakefield Cycle and was working on *The Construction of Christian Poetry in Old English* and a revision of his study of Chaucer, which he later divided into *The Life and Times of Chaucer* and *The Poetry of Chaucer*. In December Knopf published *Nickel Mountain*, a popular novel in America and in Europe, where it has been translated into at least seven languages.

1974

Though alternating productively between revisions of the title novella for *The King's Indian* and *The Life and Times of Chaucer*, Gardner was profoundly distracted by the terminal illness of his close friend Nicholas Vergette, who died on 21 February. In August Gardner taught for the first time at the Bread Loaf Writers' Conference. On 29 August *The Construction of the Wakefield Cycle* was published. From 8 September to 5 October he toured Japan in behalf of the United States Information Service. Upon his return he accepted a Hadley Fellowship at Bennington College for the academic year 1974–75. During this period he began "Shadows," a novel about an alcoholic detective in Carbondale, Illinois, and polished some of the children's stories that he had given his family at past Christmases. By early November he had readied *Dragon, Dragon* for publication. The year ended with the publication of *The King's Indian* on 5 December.

1975

By early February Gardner had bought a house in Old Bennington, where, shortly after, he began *October Light*, his "bicentennial novel." Though still holding tenure at Southern Illinois University, and though he would later return periodically to hold seminars on creative writing, he had not resided there for any significant length of time after September 1974. On 12 May *The Construction of Christian Poetry in Old English* was published. On 21 May he was elected to membership in the American Academy of Arts and Letters. In the meantime he worked on radio plays for National Public Radio: "The Temptation Game" (taped for broadcast on *Earplay:* January 1978 to July 1980) and "The Water Horse" (bought by *Earplay* for production in either 1979 or 1980). By September he had completed a session at Bread Loaf and returned again to *October Light*.

1976

By mid-February he had completed his final revision of *October Light*. By 15 August he had completed *In the Suicide Mountains* and had begun his tenure at Bread Loaf. In 1965 he had written an antiexistentialist manifesto on fiction. He now began to revise and expand it extensively, giving it the title *On Moral Fiction*. In late August he resigned his professorship at Southern Illinois University. In early October he left his wife, Joan, and moved to Cambridge, New York. On 11 October *Gudgekin the Thistle Girl* was published. Meanwhile, Gardner was submitting essays from *On Moral Fiction* to *Critical Inquiry, Hudson Review, Saturday Review*, and *Western Humanities Review*, and further heightening the controversy over his criticism of recent fiction by reading papers on the subject at various colleges and universities. *October Light* was published 6 December. Like *The Sunlight*

Dialogues and *Nickel Mountain*, it was adopted by book clubs and was a best seller.

1977

October Light won the National Book Critics Circle Award for Fiction in 1976. After receiving his award on 13 January, Gardner returned to his hectic schedule of teaching, on alternate days, the spring semester at two colleges: Skidmore and Williams. Eight days later, on 21 January, *Rumpelstiltskin*, an opera for which he wrote the libretto, was produced—Gardner in attendance—at Lexington, Kentucky. Meanwhile, he was working alternately on two novels: "Shadows" and "Rage." Then, finally, his study of Chaucer, first drafted at San Francisco State in 1963, was published: *The Poetry of Chaucer*, by Southern Illinois University Press, on 18 March; *The Life and Times of Chaucer*, by Knopf, on 5 April. From 10 June to 2 July Gardner attended the symposium on American literature at Salzburg, Austria, where he gave three lectures. In August he taught at Bread Loaf. In September he accepted a position as writer in residence at George Mason University and began to plan a series of radio shows on the arts. By mid-October he had published two children's books: *A Child's Bestiary* and *In the Suicide Mountains*. By November he had completed *On Moral Fiction*. Then, suddenly, his creative momentum was halted. On 10 December he entered Johns Hopkins Hospital for cancer surgery and stayed for six weeks. It was, he said later, his first "vacation" from writing since childhood. But it was a working vacation, apparently, for even though he did not write fiction, he did write while in the hospital, and afterward while recuperating with his Vermont friends the VanderEls, a book on how to write fiction. Tentatively called "The Art of Fiction," it reflects his twenty-five years as a teacher and writer.

1978

In the meantime his reputation was catching up with him. A profile entitled "John Gardner" was broadcast as part of a series entitled *The Originals: The Writer in America* (PBS-TV, 3 April). Then, in response to the publication of *On Moral Fiction* (19 April), he was interviewed on the *Dick Cavett Show* (PBS-TV, 16 May). On 24 May he delivered a paper entitled "Literature in Disguise: Honesty and Technique" at a meeting of the international P.E.N. organization in Stockholm, Sweden. In August he taught at Bread Loaf. In September his memorial poem "Nicholas Vergette 1923–1974" was published as a broadside by the Lord John Press, and he joined the English faculty of the State University of New York at Binghamton. On 10 November *Poems* was published by the Lord John Press. On 26 December *Rumpelstiltskin* had its professional premiere by The Opera Company of Philadelphia, and annual Christmas season performances were planned. The year ended with the announcement by the New London Press of the imminent publication of *Rumpelstiltskin* and two other libretti: *Frankenstein* and *William Wilson*.

1979

The year began with the announcement of still more publications from New London Press. Forthcoming in late 1979 are *John Gardner: An Interview; Death and the Maiden* (a play); and *The Temptation Game* (a radio play). Projected for 1980 are a one-volume edition reprinting the best of *MSS*; a libretto: "Samson and the Witch"; two radio plays: "The Angel" and "The Water Horse"; a one-volume edition uniting these two plays with *The Temptation Game*. Projected for 1981 are two plays: "Helen at Home" and "The Latest Word from Delphi"; and a libretto: "The Pied Piper of Hamlin." Meanwhile, by August 1979, Gardner had completed "Vlemk: The Box-Painter" for the Lord John Press (November 1979); "Freddy's Book" for Knopf (March 1980); a radio play for *Earplay*; and two film treatments: "The Age of Reason," for producer Sandra Marsh; and "Boswell: The London Journal," Part I, a pilot film for a proposed PBS-TV series on the Boswell journals.

John Gardner

THE OLD MEN

by

John C. Gardner, Jr.

A thesis submitted in partial fulfillment of the
requirements for the degree of Doctor of
Philosophy, in the Department of English
in the Graduate College of the State
University of Iowa

August, 1958

Chairman: Assistant Professor Ralph Freedman

It was the literary approach of one hundred thirty-seven studies that examined his work as an artistic dramatization of a personal world view which provided the most compact and meaningful appraisal of his style and themes. The forty-eight articles of miscellaneous approaches, notable chiefly for their general misrepresentations and factual inaccuracies, at least indicated Green's eminence in contemporary letters.

Among those French writers born between 1895 and 1900 (Montherlant, Giono, Malraux, etc.), Green's view of man's fate is one of the most pessimistic, since it accepts as real malicious supernatural powers. Unlike most of his colleagues, he has deliberately divorced his stories from current socio-political issues. Unlike some of them, he has concentrated as much upon lucid, syntactically-conventional form as upon the subject matter. Thus, his stressing of formal excellence will probably cause his works to be enjoyed long after those of his more "engaged" fellow writers have passed from fashion.

Microfilm $3.10; Xerox $10.60. 237 pages.

THE OLD MEN
(L. C. Card No. Mic 58-5820)
John Champlin Gardner, Jr., Ph.D.
State University of Iowa, 1958

Chairman: Assistant Professor Ralph Freedman

The Old Men is a novel which takes as its general theme the place of man in the universe and attempts to work out the nature and ramifications of man's two essential choices, affirmation and denial. It considers some of the forces latent in man's condition as spiritually perceptive animal, and explores the way these forces tend to make man's choice of either affirmation or denial necessary. Through the juxtaposition of slightly or sharply distorted internal visions of reality, normative vision becomes dependent on character relationships and agreement of various distortions. The most important of these distortions is developed from a ghost legend well enough known to all important characters in the novel to provide objectification of guilt, on one hand, and anguish, as Sartre uses the word, on the other.

The novel's setting is a backwater university town in the Catskills. Central characters are Ginger Ghoki, a sixteen-year-old who seeks spiritual involvement with the universe and ignores all restrictions for her mystical objective, and Jay Corby, a college student who seeks not involvement but detachment. Other characters fall into groups. The first group includes the "old men" of the novel, Professors Lorward, Utt, and Dean Woodstock, the girl's father Sam Ghoki, and the farmer Mr Mullen. These, the observers, present on lower planes the psychological, social, and, especially, moral awareness embodied in the novel's ghost, the long-dead minister, Lawrence Leigh. Other characters are Professors Jack Rosen and Dale Corby, each trapped (one in the present, one in the past) between affirmation and denial; Mrs Woodstock and Leta Corby, two irresponsible life-affirmers whose effect is destructive, mirroring Ginger Ghoki's story; and various highschool and college students.

The main plot concerns Ginger Ghoki who has determined, when the novel opens, to live widly and fully, unlike her rigidly moral father. She becomes emotionally involved with all of the characters in the novel and sexually involved with two, setting off rivalries and jealousies which, directly or indirectly, lead to a series of violent encounters and even deaths. The ultimate result is that Ginger, who began as a life affirmer, totally irresponsible through cosmic inclusiveness of responsibility, becomes morally responsible, and Jay Corby, the most important of the characters drawn into Ginger's story, who begins as a life denier, irresponsible through detachment and becomes, like Ginger, responsible.

Microfilm $8.60; Xerox $30.50. 678 pages.

FORMAL EXPERIMENTS IN
MODERN VERSE DRAMA
(L. C. Card No. Mic 58-7068)
Donna Lorine Gerstenberger, Ph.D.
The University of Oklahoma, 1958

Major Professor: Stanley K. Coffman, Jr.

Modern verse drama has been neglected by students of contemporary literature because of the association of verse drama with the conventional idea of nineteenth-century poetic drama as a highly specialized form using a heroic subject matter, an elevated language and artificial rhythms, and a conventional dramatic structure. Although contemporary verse dramas are still written in this manner, there has been a sustained attempt, worthy of recognition, to reclaim verse drama as a living, vital form, and this impetus in our century has come primarily from the influence of modern poets who have tried to conceive a verse drama capable of meeting the standard set for modern poetry of a totally relevant and coherent relationship in an between language, structure, and content. This revitalization of verse drama has largely been made possible by the emphasis of modern literature on structure and by its awareness of the role of language as an important (perhaps even as the fundamental) formal element in a total artistic expression. This new emphasis has made available a concept of formal integration of language and structure which had been lost to the verse stage since the Restoration. Modern poetry has supplied the idiom, the rhythms, and some structural hints. Specifically dramatic means of expression have been adapted either from the past (the Japanese Noh play, the Elizabethan or classical drama), from the modern prose theater, or from other living contemporary sources including the music hall, the ballet, and the liturgy.

The poet-playwrights examined in this study (W. B. Yeats, T. S. Eliot, W. H. Auden and Christopher Isherwood, Stephen Spender, and Christopher Fry) all work from this common awareness of the formal problem as central to a reinstatement of the verse play as a living drama; but, by and large, they approach the problem from individual points of view and techniques. The very variety of the experiments in verse drama in this century argues a renewed interest in and a renewed vitality for verse drama, and these factors make modern verse drama worthy of the

The items following each abstract are: the number of manuscript pages in the dissertation and its cost on microfilm.
Enlargements 5-1/2 x 8-1/2 inches, 4 cents per page. No postage is charged if check or money order accompanies order.

A. Separate Publications

Books, pamphlets, broadsides, and sheets wholly or substantially by Gardner, arranged chronologically, with foreign translations listed as an AA supplement at the end of the work's history.

A.I *The Old Men* (1959)

[Ann Arbor: University Microfilms, 1959]. A novel submitted as a Ph.D. dissertation by "John C. Gardner" at the State University of Iowa, August 1958. Xerox and microfilm copies of this dissertation are distributed on request by University Microfilms. The original typescript is shelved in the university library.

John Gardner *and* **Lennis Dunlap**

Chico State College

The Forms of Fiction

. . . nothing can permanently please,
which does not contain in itself
the reason why it is so,
and not otherwise.

SAMUEL TAYLOR COLERIDGE

 RANDOM HOUSE *New York*

To
Professor
Harold
C. Armstrong

FIRST PRINTING

© COPYRIGHT, 1962, BY RANDOM HOUSE, INC.

ALL RIGHTS RESERVED UNDER INTERNATIONAL AND PAN-AMERICAN
COPYRIGHT CONVENTIONS. PUBLISHED IN NEW YORK BY
RANDOM HOUSE, INC., AND SIMULTANEOUSLY IN TORONTO, CANADA,
BY RANDOM HOUSE OF CANADA, LIMITED.

LIBRARY OF CONGRESS CATALOG CARD NUMBER: 62-10780

MANUFACTURED IN THE UNITED STATES OF AMERICA

A.II *The Forms of Fiction* (1962). Edition with Commentaries by John
Gardner and Lennis Dunlap

1a New York: Random House. Hard cover, no dust wrapper. Trim
size: 13.8 x 20.9 cm. Collation: [1–21]¹⁶. [i–iv] v–vii [viii] ix–x [1–2]
3–19 [20–22] 23–187 [188–90] 191–319 [320–22] 323–657 [658–62].
Contents: 30 short stories and novellas. With Dunlap, Gardner
wrote the following commentaries: "Foreword" (v–vii); "Introduction: Reading Fiction" (3–19); "The Modern Writer's Use of
the Sketch, Fable, Yarn, and Tale" (23–37); " 'After the Storm':
Analysis" (48–50); " 'Wakefield': Questions and Comments"
(60–62); " 'A Country Doctor': Analysis" (68–73); " 'Death in the
Woods': Questions and Comments" (90–91); " 'Spotted Horses':
Analysis" (108–12); " 'Sorrow-Acre': Questions and Comments"
(155–58); " 'The Gentleman from San Francisco': Analysis"
(179–81); " 'The Blue Hotel': Questions and Comments" (354–57);
" 'The Fox': Questions and Comments" (521–24). Available: May
1962. Published: May 1962. Publication: 10, 138 copies of the first
printing. Locations: JG, JH, DLC.
1b New York: Random House, [August 1964]. Source: publisher's
archivist.
1c New York: Random House, [May 1965]. Source: publisher's
archivist.
1d New York: Random House, [October 1965]. Source: publisher's
archivist.
1e New York: Random House, [September 1966]. Source: publisher's archivist.
1f New York: Random House, [January 1967]. Location: JH.
1g New York: Random House, [June 1967]. Source: publisher's
archivist. Out of print as of February 1975.

THE COMPLETE WORKS OF
THE GĀWĀIN=POET

In a Modern English Version with a Critical Introduction
by John Gardner

Woodcuts by Fritz Kredel

THE UNIVERSITY OF CHICAGO PRESS
Chicago & London

Library of Congress Catalog Card Number: 65-17291

THE UNIVERSITY OF CHICAGO PRESS, CHICAGO & LONDON
THE UNIVERSITY OF TORONTO PRESS, TORONTO 5, CANADA

© *1965 by The University of Chicago. All rights reserved*
Published 1965
Printed in the United States of America

Designed by Adrian Wilson

A.III *The Complete Works of the Gawain-Poet in a Modern English Version with a Critical Introduction by John Gardner* (1965). Woodcuts by Fritz Kredel

1a Chicago and London: University of Chicago Press. Hard cover, dust wrapper. Trim size: 16.0 x 23.5 cm. Collation: [1–9]^{16} [10]^8 [11–12]^{16}. (First leaf is a pastedown.) [i–vi] vii–xii [xiii–xiv] [1–2] 3–90 [91–94] 95–145 [146–48] 149–200 [201–2] 203–19 [220–22] 223–324 [325–26] 327–37 [338] 339–47 [348–52]. Contents: Introduction and Commentary: "The Poet" (3); "Conventions and Traditions in the Poems" (13); "The *Gawain*-Poet's Vision of Reality" (37); "The Poet's Dramatic Sense" (42); "The Pearl Group: Interpretation" (50); "Versification and Form" (85); The Poems: "*Pearl*" (95); "*Purity*" (149); "*Patience*" (203); "*Sir Gawain and the Green Knight*" (223); "*St. Erkenwald*" (327). Available: 27 July 1965. Published: 31 August 1965. Publication: 3,000 copies of the first printing. Locations: JG, SIU-C.
1b Chicago and London: University of Chicago Press, [19 July 1967]. Source: publisher's archivist.
1c Carbondale and Edwardsville: Southern Illinois University Press; London and Amsterdam: Feffer & Simons, [19 November 1970]. Wrappers. Arcturus Paperbacks. No. AB 78. This offset printing was reduced in size.
1d Chicago and London: University of Chicago Press, [31 July 1975]. Source: publisher's archivist.
1e Chicago and London: University of Chicago Press, [28 October 1975]. Wrappers. Source: publisher's archivist.

The
Resurrection

a novel by

John Gardner

The New American Library

First Printing

Published by The New American Library, Inc.
1301 Avenue of the Americas, New York, New York 10019
Published simultaneously in Canada by General Publishing
Company, Ltd.

Library of Congress Catalog Card Number: 66–19514

Printed in the United States of America

A.IV *The Resurrection* (1966)

1a New York: New American Library. Hard cover, dust wrapper. Trim size: 13.7 x 21.0 cm. Collation: [1–8]^{16}. [i–x] 1–3 [4–6] 7–70 [71–72] 73–165 [166–68] 169–241 [242–46]. Available: 5 May 1966. Published: 20 June 1966. Publication: 2,500 copies of the first printing. Locations: JG, JH.

1b New York: New American Library [October 1966]. Source: publisher's archivist.

2a New York: Ballantine, [April 1974]. Wrappers. No. 23881. Locations: JG, JH. This edition incorporates at least 554 changes (by Gardner) of diction and punctuation.

2b Toronto: Ballantine Books of Canada, [April 1974]. Wrappers. Copyright page: "Printed in Canada."

2c New York: Ballantine, [May 1974]. Wrappers. Source: publisher's archivist.

LE MORTE DARTHUR

NOTES

including
Introduction
Life of Malory
Malory and the Legend of Arthur
The Characters
Summaries and Commentaries
Review Questions
Selected Bibliography

by
John Gardner, Ph.D.
Department of English
Southern Illinois University

consulting editor
James L. Roberts, Ph.D.
Department of English
University of Nebraska

BETHANY STATION • LINCOLN, NEBRASKA 68505

A.V *Le Morte Darthur   Notes* (1967)

1a Lincoln: Cliff's Notes. Wrappers. Trim size: 13.2 x 20.9 cm.
Collation: 40 leaves, stapled twice at center. [1–4] 5–80. Available:
22 March 1967. Published 8 May 1967. Publication: 10,000 copies
of the first printing. Locations: JG, JH.
1b Lincoln: Cliff's Notes, [November 1968]. Wrappers. Source:
publisher's archivist.
1c Lincoln: Cliff's Notes, [October 1969]. Wrappers. Source: publisher's archivist.
1d Lincoln: Cliff's Notes, [September 1971]. Wrappers. Source:
publisher's archivist.
1e Lincoln: Cliff's Notes, [August 1974]. Wrappers. Source: publisher's archivist.

THE GAWAIN-POET

NOTES

Notes on *Pearl* and *Sir Gawain and the Green Knight*, with brief commentary on *Purity* and *Patience*.

including
A Note on the Text
A Note on Interpretation and
   the Use of This Volume
Introduction
Language and Style
Summaries and Commentaries
Review Questions
Selected Bibliography

by
John Gardner, Ph.D.
Department of English
Southern Illinois University

consulting editor
James L. Roberts, Ph.D.
Department of English
University of Nebraska

BETHANY STATION • LINCOLN, NEBRASKA 68505

A.VI *The Gawain-Poet Notes* (1967)

1a Lincoln: Cliff's Notes. Wrappers. Trim size: 13.2 x 20.9 cm.
Collation: 40 leaves, stapled twice at center. [1–4] 5–78 [79–80].
Available: 8 August 1967. Published: 20 October 1967. Publication: 6,000 copies of the first printing. Locations: JG, JH.
1b Lincoln: Cliff's Notes, [February 1968]. Wrappers. Source: publisher's archivist.
1c Lincoln: Cliff's Notes, [March 1969]. Wrappers. Source: publisher's archivist.
1d Lincoln: Cliff's Notes, [June 1970]. Wrappers. Source: publisher's archivist.
1e Lincoln: Cliff's Notes, [August 1971]. Wrappers. Source: publisher's archivist.
1f Lincoln: Cliff's Notes, [March 1972]. Wrappers. Source: publisher's archivist.
1g Lincoln: Cliff's Notes, [December 1972]. Wrappers. Source: publisher's archivist.
1h Lincoln: Cliff's Notes, [December 1973]. Wrappers. Source: publisher's archivist.
1i Lincoln: Cliff's Notes, [August 1974]. Wrappers. Source: publisher's archivist.
1j Lincoln: Cliff's Notes, [February 1976]. Wrappers. Source: publisher's archivist.

THE WRECKAGE OF AGATHON

John Gardner

HARPER & ROW, PUBLISHERS

NEW YORK, EVANSTON, AND LONDON

A.VII *The Wreckage of Agathon* (1970)

1a New York, Evanston, and London: Harper & Row. Hard cover, dust wrapper. Trim size: 14.0 x 20.5 cm. Collation: [1–8]¹⁶. [i–viii] 1–243 [244–48]. Available: 26 June 1970. Published: 23 September 1970. Publication: 6,500 copies of the first printing. Locations: JG, JH, SIU-C.

2a New York: Ballantine, [January 1972]. Wrappers. No. 22472. Source: publisher's archivist.

2b New York: Ballantine, [December 1973]. Wrappers. Locations: JG, JH. This printing was also distributed in a boxed set with *Grendel* and *The Sunlight Dialogues*. Slipcase. No. 23684.

2c New York: Ballantine, [February 1974]. Wrappers. Source: publisher's archivist.

2d Middletown, Pa.: Quality Paperback Book Club, [7 February 1975]. Wrappers. Source: publisher's archivist. This printing was distributed in a boxed set with *Grendel* and *The Sunlight Dialogues* and is identical to Ballantine's slipcased collection except for the omission of price.

AA.VII Translations

Le naufrage d'Agathon. Trans. Anne Villelaur. Paris: Denoël, 1973. 284 pages.

Upadek Agatona. Trans. Natalia Billi. Preface by Zygmunt Kubiak, on pp. 7–10. Warsaw: Czytelnik, 1976. 330 pages.

JOHN GARDNER

GRENDEL

Illustrated by Emil Antonucci

Alfred A. Knopf · New York · 1971

THIS IS A BORZOI BOOK
PUBLISHED BY ALFRED A. KNOPF, INC.

Copyright © 1971 by John Gardner
All rights reserved under International and Pan-American
Copyright Conventions. Published in the United States
by Alfred A. Knopf, Inc., New York, and simultaneously
in Canada by Random House of Canada Limited, Toronto.
Distributed by Random House, Inc., New York.
ISBN: 0-394-47143-1
Library of Congress Catalog Card Number: 70-154911
Manufactured in the United States of America

FIRST EDITION

My thanks to Thomas Kinsella for permission
to use his poem *Wormwood*.

A.VIII *Grendel* (1971). Illustrated by Emil Antonucci

1a New York: Knopf. Hard cover, dust wrapper. Trim size: 14.0 x
21.0 cm. Collation: [1–6]¹⁶. [i–xii] [1–4] 5–174 [175–80]. Illustrations: Full page: [vi], [3]. Half page: 5, 15, 30, 46, 57, 75, 91, 111,
125, 138, 151, 167. Available: 24 June 1971. Published: 17 September 1971. Publication: 7,500 copies of the first printing.
Locations: JG, JH, SIU-C. Listed as one of the year's best novels
by *Time* and *Newsweek*. Joint winner of the book of the year award
given by The Conference on Christianity and Literature. "The
Song of Grendel," an excerpt, appeared in *Esquire* (see C.8).
1b New York: Knopf, [October 1971]. Source: publisher's archivist.
1c New York; Knopf, [January 1972]. Source: publisher's archivist.
1d New York: Knopf, [May 1972]. Source: publisher's archivist.
1e London: Deutsch, [26 June 1972]. Location: JG.
1f New York: Knopf, [November 1972]. Source: publisher's archivist.
1g New York: Knopf, [May 1973]. Source: publisher's archivist.
1h New York: Knopf, [September 1976]. Source: publisher's archivist.
2a Boston: G. K. Hall, [March 1972]. Locations: JG, JH. This was a
large print edition.
3a New York: Ballantine, [October 1972]. Wrappers. No. 25076.
Locations: JG, JH.
3b New York: Ballantine, [November 1972]. Wrappers. Source:
publisher's archivist.
3c New York: Ballantine, [March 1973]. Wrappers. Source: publisher's archivist.
3d New York: Ballantine, [March 1973]. Wrappers. Source: publisher's archivist.
3e New York: Ballantine, [September 1973]. Wrappers. Source:
publisher's archivist.
3f New York: Ballantine, [December 1973]. Wrappers. Locations:
JG, JH. This printing was also distributed in a boxed set with *The
Wreckage of Agathon* and *The Sunlight Dialogues*. Slipcase. No.
23684.
3g New York: Ballantine, [May 1974]. Wrappers. Source: publisher's
archivist.
3h New York: Ballantine, [October 1974]. Wrappers. Source: publisher's archivist.
3i Middletown, Pa.: Quality Paperback Book Club. [7 February

1975]. Wrappers. Source: publisher's archivist. This printing was distributed in a boxed set with *The Wreckage of Agathon* and *The Sunlight Dialogues* and is identical to Ballantine's slipcased collection, except for the omission of price.

3j New York: Ballantine, [November 1975]. Wrappers. Source: publisher's archivist.

3k New York: Ballantine, [August 1976]. Wrappers. Source: publisher's archivist.

3l New York: Ballantine, [January 1977]. Wrappers. Source: publisher's archivist.

3m New York: Ballantine, [November 1977]. Wrappers. Source: publisher's archivist.

4a London: Pan, [12 October 1973]. Wrappers. Picador edition. Locations: JG, JH.

AA.VIII Translations

Grendel. Trans. René Daillie. Preface by Max-Pol Fouchet, pp. [11]–18. Introduction by John Gardner, pp. [19]–23. Afterword by translator, pp. [191]–204. Original illustrations. Paris: Denoël, 1974. 204 pages. See B.6.

Grendel. Trans. Camila Batlles Barcelona: Ediciones Destino, 1975. 190 pages.

Grendel. Trans. Reidar Ekner. Afterword by the translator, pp. 127–[130]. Stockholm: Pan/Norstedts, 1975. 130 pages.

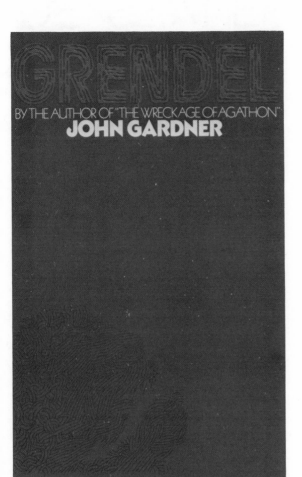

GRENDEL

BY THE AUTHOR OF "THE WRECKAGE OF AGATHON"
JOHN GARDNER

THE ALLITERATIVE
MORTE ARTHURE
The Owl and the Nightingale

AND FIVE OTHER
MIDDLE ENGLISH POEMS

in a Modernized Version with

Comments on the Poems

and Notes

By John Gardner

SOUTHERN ILLINOIS UNIVERSITY PRESS
Carbondale and Edwardsville

FEFFER & SIMONS, INC.
London and Amsterdam

COPYRIGHT © *1971 by Southern Illinois University Press*
All rights reserved
Printed in the United States of America
Designed by Andor Braun
ISBN 0-8093-0486-4
Library of Congress Catalog Card Number 76-139284

A.IX *The Alliterative Morte Arthure   The Owl and the Nightingale   And Five Other Middle English Poems in a Modernized Version with Comments on the Poems and Notes* (1971)

1a Carbondale and Edwardsville: Southern Illinois University Press; London and Amsterdam: Feffer & Simons. Hard cover, dust wrapper. Trim size: 15.2 x 23.7 cm. Collation: [1–10]^{16}. (First leaf is a pastedown) [i–vi] vii–xi [xiii] [1–2] 3–113 [114–16] 117–30 [131–32] 133–51 [152–54] 155–58 [159–60] 161–73 [174–76] 177–82 [183–84] 185–231 [232–34] 235–98 [299–306]. Contents: "The Alliterative Morte Arthur" (3); "Winner and Waster" (117); "The Parliament of the Three Ages" (133); "Summer Sunday" (155); "The Debate of Body and Soul" (161); "The Thrush and the Nightingale" (177); "The Owl and the Nightingale" (185); "Comments on the Poems" (267). Available: 9 September 1971. Published: 27 September 1971. Publication: 1,547 copies of the first printing. Locations: JG, JH, SIU-C.
1b Carbondale and Edwardsville: Southern Illinois University Press; London and Amsterdam: Feffer & Simons, [27 September 1973]. Wrappers. Arcturus Paperbacks. No. AB 116. This offset printing was reduced in size.

THE
SUNLIGHT
DIALOGUES

John Gardner

ILLUSTRATIONS BY JOHN NAPPER

1972 · ALFRED A. KNOPF · NEW YORK

THIS IS A BORZOI BOOK
PUBLISHED BY ALFRED A. KNOPF, INC.

Copyright © 1972 by John Gardner
All rights reserved under International and Pan-American Copyright Conventions.
Published in the United States by Alfred A. Knopf, Inc., New York, and simultaneously
in Canada by Random House of Canada Limited, Toronto.
Distributed by Random House, Inc., New York.

Library of Congress Cataloging in Publication Data

Gardner, John Champlin, 1933-
The sunlight dialogues.

I. Title.
PZ4.G23117Su   [PS3557.A712]   813'.5'4   72-2226
ISBN 0-394-47144-X

Manufactured in the United States of America
First Edition

A.X *The Sunlight Dialogues* (1972). Illustrated by John Napper

1a New York: Knopf. Hard cover, dust wrapper. Trim size: 15.6 x
23.6 cm. Collation: [1–20]^{16} [21]^8 [22–23]^{16}. (First leaf is a
pastedown.) [i–ix] x [xi] xii [xiii] xiv–xvi [xvii–xviii] [1–3] 4–5
[6–7] 8–46 [2 pp.] 47–58 [59] 60–96 [2 pp.] 97–123 [124] 125–78 [179]
180–86 [2 pp.] 187–207 [208] 209–52 [2 pp.] 253–74 [275] 276–96 [2
pp.] 297–301 [302] 303–14 [2 pp.] 315–30 [331] 332–57 [358] 359–84
[2 pp.] 385–99 [400] [2 pp.] 401–28 [429] 430–49 [450] 451–84 [485]
486–500 [2 pp.] 501–6 [507] 508–30 [2 pp.] 531–36 [537] 538–44 [545]
546–64 [565] 566–74 [2 pp.] 575–76 [577] 578–610 [611] 612–24 [625]
626–34 [635] 636–42 [643] 644–64 [2 pp.] 665–66 [667] 668–73
[674–76]. Illustrations: [iv]; facing 46, 96, 186, 252, 296, 314, 384,
[400], 500, 530, 574, 664. The "Certificate of Death" [674] was
filled in by the author. Available: 19 October 1972. Published: 6
December 1972. Publication: 8,775 copies of the first printing.
Locations: JG, JH, SIU-C. John Napper published an additional
set of illustrations in portfolio (see B.8). See also C.3.

1b New York: Knopf, [December 1972]. Source: publisher's archivist.

1c New York: Knopf, [January 1973]. Source: publisher's archivist.
This printing was also apparently distributed by the American
Journal Book Club, [4 June 1973], now defunct. Though the
details of publication are presently unavailable, the speculation is
that the club's copies were printed and bound along with Knopf's
and are identical to the Knopf printing.

1d New York: Knopf, [February 1973]. Source: publisher's archivist.

1e New York: Knopf, [March 1973]. Source: publisher's archivist.

1f New York: Knopf, [May 1973]. Source: publisher's archivist.

1g New York: Knopf, [August 1976]. Source: publisher's archivist.

2a New York: Literary Guild, [March 1973]. Location: SIU-C. This
edition was reduced in size (13.2 x 20.8 cm); lengthened (710
numbered pages); and distinguished by the imprint "Book Club
Edition" on the front flap.

1h London: Cape, [11 October 1973]. Location: British Museum.

3a New York: Ballantine, [December 1973]. Wrappers. No. 23650.
Locations: JG, JH.

3b New York: Ballantine, [December 1973]. Slipcase. No. 23684.
Locations: JG, JH. Distributed with *The Wreckage of Agathon* and
Grendel. The copyright page lists this as a "Second printing."

3c New York: Ballantine, [April 1974]. Source: publisher's archivist.

3d Middletown, Pa.: Quality Paperback Book Club, [7 February 1975]. Slipcase. Source: publisher's archivist. Distributed in a boxed set with *The Wreckage of Agathon* and *Grendel*. Identical to Ballantine's slipcased collection except for the omission of price.

AA.X Translations

De duivelbanner. Trans. Lore Coutinho. Amsterdam: Uitgeverij De Arbeiderspers, 1975. 686 pages.

L'Homme-Soleil. Trans. Claude and Anny Mourthé. Paris: Denoël, 1974. 648 pages.

Der Ruhestörer oder Die Gespräche mit dem Sonnen-Mann. Trans. Hermann Stiehl. Hamburg: Rowohlt, 1977. 668 pages.

Soldialogerna. Trans. Thomas Preis. Stockholm: Norstedts, 1979. 344 pages.

The Sunlight Dialogues

A Novel by
John Gardner
Illustrated by
John Napper

Alfred A. Knopf

JASON
AND
MEDEIA

JOHN GARDNER

ALFRED A. KNOPF
New York
1973

THIS IS A BORZOI BOOK
PUBLISHED BY ALFRED A. KNOPF, INC.

Library of Congress Cataloging in Publication Data

Gardner, John Champlin, (date)
    Jason and Medeia.

    1. Jason—Romances. 2. Medea—Romances.
I. Title.
PS3557.A712J3   811'.5'4   72-11021
ISBN 0-394-48337-0

Manufactured in the United States of America

FIRST EDITION

A.XI *Jason and Medeia* (1973). Classical Illustrations

1a New York: Knopf. Hard cover, dust wrapper. Trim size: 15.8 x
   23.5 cm. Collation: [1–10]¹⁶ [11]⁸ [12]¹⁶. [i–xii] [1–2] 3–16 [17] 18–29
   [30] 31–43 [44] 45–54 [55] 56–65 [66] 67–88 [89] 90–107 [108–9]
   110–19 [120]121–33 [134] 135–44 [145] 146–57 [158] 159–71 [172]
   173–84 [185] 186–205 [206–7] 208–19 [220–21] 222–35 [236] 237–54
   [255] 256–70 [271] 272–83 [284] 285–303 [304] 305–14 [315] 316–27
   [328] 329–42 [343] 344–54 [355–56]. Full-page illustrations: [iv],
   [2],[17], [30], [44], [55], [66], [89], [108–9], [120], [134], [145], [158],
   [172], [185], [206–7], [220–21], [236], [255], [271], [284], [304],
   [315], [328], [343], [355–56]. Available: 22 May 1973. Published: 21
   June 1973. Publication: 7,500 copies of the first printing. Locations: JG, JH, SIU-C. "Lemnos" first appeared in *Fiction Midwest*
   (see D.18).
1b New York: Knopf, [August 1973]. Source: publisher's archivist.
2a New York: Ballantine, [February 1975]. Wrappers. No. 24418.
   Locations: JG, JH. Illustrations were dropped from this edition.

NICKEL MOUNTAIN

A PASTORAL NOVEL

JOHN GARDNER

WITH ETCHINGS BY THOMAS O'DONOHUE

ALFRED A. KNOPF   NEW YORK   1973

THIS IS A BORZOI BOOK
PUBLISHED BY ALFRED A. KNOPF, INC.

Copyright © 1963, 1966, 1971, 1972, 1973 by John Gardner
All rights reserved under
International and Pan-American Copyright Conventions.
Published in the United States by Alfred A. Knopf, Inc., New York,
and simultaneously in Canada by Random House of Canada Limited,
Toronto. Distributed by Random House, Inc., New York.

Library of Congress Cataloging in Publication Data

Gardner, John Champlin, (date)
Nickel mountain.

I. Title.
PZ4.G23117Ni [PS3557.A712]   813'.5'4   73-7293
ISBN 0-394-48883-0

Portions of this book have appeared in *Quarterly Review of Literature*,
The Southern Review and *Perspective*.

Manufactured in the United States of America
First Edition

A.XII *Nickel Mountain   A Pastoral Novel* (1973). Illustrated by Thomas O'Donohue

1a New York: Knopf. Hard cover, dust wrapper. [Title page: dark orange background; stop-press adjustment: light orange background.] Trim size: 14.2 x 21.1 cm. Collation: $[1-5]^{16}[6]^{12}[7-11]^{16}$. [i–xii] [1–3] 4–22 [2 pp.] 23–59 [60–63] 64–84 [2 pp.] [85–87] 88–90 [2 pp.] 91–123 [124–27] 128–34 [2 pp.] 135–41 [142–45] 146–90 [2 pp.] 191–208 [209–11] 212–30 [2 pp.] 231–62 [263–65] 266–88 [2 pp.] 289–90 [291–93] 294–312 [313–18]. Illustrations: [vi]; facing 22, 84, 90, 134, 190, 230, 288, 312. Available: 3 December 1973. Published: 3 December 1973. Publication: 27,500 copies of the first printing. Locations: JG, JH, SIU-C. Some of the chapters are variants of published stories (see C.2, C.4, C.5, C.6, C.7, C.10); a condensation of the novel was published in *Redbook* magazine (see C.14).
1b New York: Knopf, [December 1973]. Source: publisher's archivist.
1c New York: Knopf, [January 1974]. Source: publisher's archivist.
1d Camp Hill, Pa.: Book-of-the-Month Club, [14 January 1974]. Source: publisher's archivist. Light tan binding; identified with a square blind-stamped on back binding.
1e New York: Knopf, [April 1974]. Source: publisher's archivist.
1f Camp Hill, Pa.: Book-of-the-Month Club, [30 April 1974]. Source: publisher's archivist.
1g London: Cape, [14 November 1974]. Without illustrations. Location: JH.
1h New Delhi: Tata McGraw-Hill, [30 December 1974]. Location: JG.
1i An unauthorized photocopy, [n.d.]. Location: JG. This photocopy of the first edition was offered for sale by Caves Books Co., 99 Chung Shan Rd. N. (2), Taipei, Taiwan.
2a New York: Ballantine, [January 1975]. Wrappers. No. 24275. Locations: JG, JH.
2b New York: Ballantine, [February 1975]. Wrappers. Source: publisher's archivist.
2c New York: Ballantine, [November 1975]. Wrappers. Source: publisher's archivist.
2d New York: Ballantine, [December 1976]. Wrappers. Source: publisher's archivist.

AA.XII Translations

Nikkelbjerget. Trans. Anne Marie Bjerg. Haslev, Denmark: Gyldendal, 1976. 233 pages.

Nikkelivuori. Trans. Jussi Nousiainen. Helsinki: Kirjayttyma, 1976. 293 pages.

A l'ombre du Mont Nickel. Trans. Anne Villelaur. Paris: Denoël, 1976. 287 pages.

A Nikkel-Hegy Pastoral. Trans. Lászlo Balazs. Budapest: Europa Konyvkiado, 1977. 254 pages.

Nikkelberget. Trans. Axel S. Seeberg. Oslo: H. Aschehoug & Co., 1976. 225 pages.

La Montaña de Niquel. Trans. Marcelo Covián. Barcelona-Buenos Aires-Mexico, D.F.: Ediciones Grijalbo, 1977. 311 pages.

Nickelberget. Trans. Annika Preis. Stockholm: Norstedts, 1975. 288 pages. Distributed as a Swedish Book of the Month.

Forthcoming or unverified: Japanese, Turkish.

Nickel
Mountain

John
Gardner

NICKEL
MOUNTAIN

JOHN GARDNER

Knopf

A novel by the author of THE SUNLIGHT DIALOGUES
Illustrated by THOMAS O'DONOHUE

The
Construction
of the
Wakefield Cycle

by JOHN GARDNER

SOUTHERN ILLINOIS UNIVERSITY PRESS
Carbondale and Edwardsville

Feffer & Simons, Inc.
London and Amsterdam

Library of Congress Cataloging in Publication Data

Gardner, John, 1933–
    The construction of the Wakefield cycle.

    (Literary structures)
    Includes bibliographical references.
    1. English drama—To 1500—History and criticism.
2. Pageants—Wakefield, England. 3. Towneley plays.
4. Mysteries and miracle—Plays, English—History and
criticism. 1. Title II. Title: Wakefield cycle.
PR644.W3G3   822'.051   74-5191
ISBN 0-8093-0665-4

A.XIII *The Construction of the Wakefield Cycle* (1974)

1a Carbondale and Edwardsville: Southern Illinois University Press; London and Amsterdam: Feffer & Simons. Hard cover, dust wrapper. Trim size: 14.8 x 22.7 cm. Collation: [1–4]¹⁶ [5]⁸ [6]¹⁶. [i–vi] vii [viii] ix [x–xii] 1–140 [141–42] 143–62 [163–64]. Available: 19 July 1974. Published: 29 August 1974. Publication: 1,483 copies of the first printing. Locations: JG, JH, SIU-C. The book is in the Literary Structures series edited by Gardner.

THE
KING'S INDIAN

Stories and Tales

JOHN GARDNER

Illustrated by Herbert L. Fink

Alfred A. Knopf · New York · 1974

THIS IS A BORZOI BOOK
PUBLISHED BY ALFRED A. KNOPF, INC.

Copyright © 1972, 1973, 1974 by John Gardner
All rights reserved under
International and Pan-American Copyright Conventions.
Published in the United States by Alfred A. Knopf, Inc., New York,
and simultaneously in Canada by Random House of Canada Limited,
Toronto. Distributed by Random House, Inc., New York.

Portions of this book originally appeared in
Audience Magazine, Fantastic, American Poetry Review, Esquire,
and Tri-Quarterly.

Library of Congress Cataloging in Publication Data

Gardner, John Champlin, date
The king's Indian.

CONTENTS: Pastoral care.—The ravages of spring.—
The temptation of St. Ivo. [etc.]
I. Title.
PZ4.G23117Ki   [PS3557.A712]   813'5'4   73-22489
ISBN 0-394-49221-8

Manufactured in the United States of America
First Edition

A.XIV *The King's Indian   Stories and Tales* (1974). Illustrated by Herbert L. Fink

1a New York: Knopf. Hard cover, dust wrapper. Trim size: 15.6 x 23.5 cm. Collation: [1–9]¹⁶ [10]⁸ [11]¹⁶. [i–x] [1–2] 3–4 [5–6] 7–36 [37–38] 39–40 [41–44] 45–60 [61–64] 65–70 [71–72] 73–82 [83–86] 87–130 [131–32] 133–34 [135–36] 137–46 [147–50] 151–58 [159–62] 163–72 [173–76] 177–94 [195–96] 197–208 [209–10] 211–28 [229–30] 231–318 [319–20] 321–23 [324–26]. Full-page illustrations: [5], [37], [42–43], [62–63], [71], [84–85], [131], [148–49], [160–61], [174–75], [209], [229], [319]. Contents: Book One: "The Midnight Reader": "Pastoral Care" (see C.11); "The Ravages of Spring" (see C.13); "The Temptation of St. Ivo" (see C.12); "The Warden" (see C.19); "John Napper Sailing Through the Universe" (see B.7); Book Two: "Tales of Queen Louisa": "Queen Louisa" (see B.17); "King Gregor and the Fool" (see C.16); "Muriel"; Book Three: "The King's Indian: A Tale." Available: 17 September 1974. Published: 5 December 1974. Publication: 7,500 copies of the first printing. Locations: JG, JH, SIU-C. Herbert Fink won the Society of Illustrators' Gold Medal Award of the year for the illustrations.
1b New York: Knopf, [November 1974]. Source: publisher's archivist.
1c London: Cape, [30 October 1975]. Without illustrations. Location: British Museum.
1d An unauthorized photocopy [n.d.]. Source: Serendipity Books. This photocopy of the first edition was offered for sale by Chin Shan Books, 89-C Chung Shan Rd. N. (2), Taipei, Taiwan.
2a New York: Ballantine, [February 1976]. Wrappers. No. 24806. Locations: JG, JH.
2b New York: Ballantine, [July 1976]. Wrappers. Source: publisher's archivist.

AA.XIV Translations

Defensa india. Trans. not listed. Original illustrations, with additional illustrations by Carlos Muleiro. Buenos Aires: Emecé Editores, 1976. 291 pages.

Kungens indian. Trans. Reidar Ekner. Stockholm: Pan/Norstedts, 1977. 187 pages.

Forthcoming or unverified: French, Japanese.

The Construction
of Christian Poetry
in Old English

by

John Gardner

SOUTHERN ILLINOIS UNIVERSITY PRESS
Carbondale and Edwardsville

Feffer & Simons, Inc.
London and Amsterdam

Library of Congress Cataloging in Publication Data
Gardner, John Champlin, 1933–
    The construction of Christian poetry in Old English.

    (Literary structures)
    Includes bibliographical references and index.
    1. Anglo-Saxon poetry—History and criticism.
    2. Christian poetry, Anglo-Saxon—History and criticism.
    I. Title.
    PR201.G37   829'.1   74-28175
    ISBN 0-8093-0705-7

A.XV *The Construction of Christian Poetry in Old English* (1975)

1a   Carbondale and Edwardsville: Southern Illinois University Press; London and Amsterdam: Feffer & Simons. Hard cover, dust wrapper. Trim size: 14.9 x 22.8 cm. Collation: [1–5]^{16}. [i–viii] ix–xii 1–120 [121–22] 123–47 [148]. Available: 3 April 1975. Published: 12 May 1975. Publication: 1,574 copies of the first printing. Locations: JG, JH, SIU-C. The book is in the Literary Structures series edited by Gardner.

JOHN GARDNER

DRAGON, DRAGON
and Other Tales

Illustrated by Charles Shields

ALFRED A. KNOPF ✑ NEW YORK

THIS IS A BORZOI BOOK PUBLISHED BY ALFRED A. KNOPF, INC.

Text Copyright © 1975 by Boskydell Artists Ltd. Illustrations Copyright © 1975 by
Charles Shields. All rights reserved under International and Pan-American Copyright
Conventions. Published in the United States by Alfred A. Knopf, Inc., New York, and
simultaneously in Canada by Random House of Canada Limited, Toronto. Distributed by
Random House, Inc., New York. Library of Congress Cataloging in Publication Data.
Gardner, John Champlin, 1933–Dragon, dragon, and other tales
SUMMARY
Four fairy tales featuring a dragon, a giant, a cunning mule, and a little chimney-girl.
1. Fairy tales. [1. Fairy tales] I. Shields, Charles. II. Title. rz8.G216Dr [398.2] 75-2542.
ISBN 0-394-83122-5. ISBN 0-394-93122-X lib. bdg. Manufactured in the United States of
America 0987654321

A.XVI *Dragon, Dragon and Other Tales* (1975). Illustrated by Charles Shields

1a New York: Knopf. Hard cover, dust wrapper; library binding. Trim size: 16.2 x 22.7 cm. Collation: [1]^{16} [2–3]^8 [4]^{16}. (First and last leaves are pastedowns.) [i–xiv] [1–2] 3–7 [8] 9–13 [14] 15–17 [18–20] 21–22 [23] 24–31 [32] 33–35 [36–38] 39–41 [42–43] 44–51 [52–53] 54 [55–56] 57–62 [63] 64–67 [68] 69–73 [74–82]. Illustrations: [8], [14], [22], [32], [42–43], [52–53], [63], [68]. Contents: "Dragon, Dragon," "The Tailor and the Giant," "The Miller's Mule," "The Last Piece of Light." Available: 19 August 1975. Published: 6 October 1975. Publication: 9,725 copies of the first printing. Locations: JG, JH, SIU-C. This book was selected as *"The New York Times Outstanding Book for Children 1975."*

1b New York: Knopf, [17 November 1975]. Source: publisher's archivist.

1c New York: Knopf, [5 February 1976]. Source: publisher's archivist.

2a New York: Bantam, [October 1976]. Wrappers. Bantam Skylark. No. 15000-6. Location: JH.

1d Camp Hill, Pa.: Book-of-the-Month Club, [September 1977]. Source: publisher's archivist. A Juvenile Dividend offered as part of a three-volume set with *Gudgekin the Thistle Girl and Other Tales* and *The King of the Hummingbirds and Other Tales.*

1e Camp Hill, Pa.: Book-of-the-Month Club, [December 1977]. Source: publisher's archivist. A Juvenile Dividend offered as part of a three-volume set with *Gudgekin the Thistle Girl and Other Tales* and *The King of the Hummingbirds and Other Tales.*

2b New York: Bantam, [October 1977]. Wrappers. Source: publisher's archivist.

2c New York: Bantam, [February 1978]. Wrappers. Source: publisher's archivist.

AA.XVI Translations

Drake, drake, hur star det till? Trans. Jadwiga P. Westrup. Stockholm: Almqvist & Wiksell, 1977. 82 pages.

Dragón, dragón y otros cuentos. Madrid: Ediciones Alfaquara, 1977. 104 pages. Unverified.

The Motorcycle Riders

On a motorcycle, man and wife
— Fat goblins, middle-aged —
rode down the roaring slopes of night:
the dark engine raged,

spit fire on curves. Black helmeted,
big-eyed as fish, they dove
down through the sleep of living and dead,
shattered the bone-white grove

and rang the smooth glass lake like a bell.
Once they too were young:
not now. Now they come to tell
how young love was wrong.

Brave boys laboring throttle and spark,
the night grove roars for you!
White-breasted ladies, you'll go dark
as other treasures do.

Like boulders rumbling by they roar
by us. She clings, serene,
and shouts in his ear. He cannot hear.
Love is obscene. Obscene.

John Gardner

a
folger poetry broadside
series 1976

A.XVII *The Motorcycle Riders* (1975)

Washington, D.C.: Folger Library Broadside Series 1976. Copyright: 1 December 1975. Broadside. Tan paper. Trim size: 21.5 x 35.5 cm. Publication: 200 copies of facsimile printed and circulated for Gardner's reading at the Folger Shakespeare Library on 1 December 1975. Location: JH. Copied out in script by Gardner from an earlier publication in *Perspective* (see D.14); reprinted (in type) in *Poems*.

JOHN GARDNER

GUDGEKIN
THE THISTLE GIRL
and Other Tales

Illustrated by Michael Sporn

ALFRED A. KNOPF 🦅 NEW YORK

To Joel and Lucy

THIS IS A BORZOI BOOK PUBLISHED BY ALFRED A. KNOPF, INC.

Text Copyright © 1976 by Boskydell Artists Ltd. Illustrations Copyright © 1976 by Michael Sporn. All rights reserved under International and Pan-American Copyright Conventions. Published in the United States by Alfred A. Knopf, Inc., New York, and simultaneously in Canada by Random House of Canada Limited, Toronto. Distributed by Random House, Inc., New York. Library of Congress Cataloging in Publication Data. Gardner, John Champlin, 1933–Gudgekin, the thistle girl, and other tales. CONTENTS: Gudgekin, the thistle girl. —The griffin and the wise old philosopher. —The Shape-Shifters of Skorm. —The sea-gulls. I. Fairy tales. [1. Fairy tales]. I. Title. PZ8.G216Go [Fic] 76-6810 ISBN 0-394-83270-0 ISBN 0-394-93270-5 lib. bdg. Manufactured in the United States of America 0987654321

A.XVIII Gudgekin the Thistle Girl and Other Tales (1976). Illustrated by
Michael Sporn

1a New York: Knopf. Hard cover, dust wrapper; library binding.
Trim size: 16.6 x 22.8 cm. Collation: [1–3]¹² (First and last leaves
are pastedowns.) [i–x] [1–2] 3–8 [9] 10–13 [14] 15–20 [21–22] 23–26
[27] 28–32 [33] 34–39 [40–42] 43–46 [47] 48–49 [50] 51–52 [53–54] 55
[56] 57–59 [60–62]. Illustrations: [4], [14], [27], [33], [46], [50], [56].
Contents: "Gudgekin the Thistle Girl," "The Griffin and the Wise
Old Philosopher," "The Shape-Shifters of Shorm," "The Sea
Gulls." Available: 15 August 1976. Published: 11 October 1976.
Publication: 12,500 copies of the first printing. Locations: JG, JH,
SIU-C.
1b New York: Junior Literary Guild, [October 1976]. Source: Literary
Guild archivist. This edition was identical to the Knopf edition,
except for the imprint of "Junior Literary Guild" on the spine of
both the binding and the dust jacket.
1c Camp Hill, Pa.: Book-of-the-Month Club, [September 1977].
Source: publisher's archivist. A Juvenile Dividend offered as part
of a three-volume set with *Dragon, Dragon and Other Tales* and
The King of the Hummingbirds and Other Tales.
1d Camp Hill, Pa.: Book-of-the-Month Club, [December 1977].
Source: publisher's archivist. A Juvenile Dividend offered as part
of a three-volume set with *Dragon, Dragon and Other Tales* and
The King of the Hummingbirds and Other Tales.
2a New York: Bantam, [February 1978]. Wrappers. Bantam Skylark.
No. 15021-9. Location: JH.

*Illustrated by Elaine Raphael
and Don Bolognese*

John Gardner

October Light

Alfred A. Knopf New York 1976

THIS IS A BORZOI BOOK
PUBLISHED BY ALFRED A. KNOPF, INC.

Copyright © 1976 by Boskydell Artists Ltd.
Illustrations Copyright © 1976 by Don Bolognese
All rights reserved under International
and Pan-American Copyright Conventions.
Published in the United States by Alfred A. Knopf, Inc., New York,
and simultaneously in Canada by Random House of Canada Limited, Toronto.
Distributed by Random House, Inc., New York.

Library of Congress Cataloging in Publication Data
Gardner, John Champlin [date]
October light.
I. Title.
PZ4.G231170c   [PS3557.A712]   813'.5'4   76-13718
ISBN 0-394-40912-3

Manufactured in the United States of America
First Edition

A.XIX *October Light* (1976). Illustrated by Elaine Raphael and Don Bolognese

1a New York: Knopf. Hard cover, dust wrapper. Trim size: 14.2 x 21.1 cm. Collation: [1–14]^{16}. [i–xii] [1–4] 5 [6] 7 [8] 9 [10] 11 [12] 13 [14] 15 [16–18] 19 [20] 21 [22] 23 [24] 25 [26] 27 [28] 29 [30] 31 [32] 33 [34] 35 [36] 37 [38] 39 [40] 41 [42] 43 [44] 45 [46] 47 [48] 49 [50] 51 [52] 53 [54] 55 [56–58] 59 [60] 61 [62] 63 [64] 65 [66] 67 [68] 69 [70] 71 [72] 73 [74] 75 [76] 77 [78] 79 [80] 81 [82] 83 [84] 85 [86] 87 [88] 89 [90] 91 [92] 93 [94] 95 [96] 97 [98] 99 [100] 101 [102] 103 [104] 105 [106] 107 [108] 109 [110] 111 [112] 113 [114] 115 [116–18] 119 [120] 121 [122] 123 [124] 125 [126] 127 [128] 129 [130] 131 [132] 133 [134] 135 [136] 137 [138–42] 143 [144] 145 [146] 147 [148] 149 [150] 151 [152] 153 [154] 155 [156] 157 [158] 159 [160] 161 [162] 163 [164] 165 [166] 167 [168] 169 [170] 171 [172] 173 [174] 175 [176] 177 [178] 179 [180] 181 [182] 183 [184–86] 187 [188] 189 [190] 191 [192] 193 [194] 195 [196] 197 [198] 199 [200] 201 [202] 203 [204] 205 [206] 207 [208–10] 211 [212] 213 [214] 215 [216] 217 [218] 219 [220] 221 [222] 223 [224] 225 [226] 227 [228] 229 [230] 231 [232] 233 [234] 235 [236] [237–42] 243 [244] 245 [246] 247 [248] 249 [250] 251 [252] 253 [254] 255 [256] 257 [258] 259 [260] 261 [262] 263 [264] 265 [266] 267 [268] 269 [270] 271 [272] 273 [274] 275 [276] 277 [278] 279 [280] 281 [282–84] 285 [286] 287 [288] 289 [290] 291 [292] 293 [294] 295 [296] 297 [298] 299 [300] 301 [302] 303 [304] 305 [306] 307 [308] 309 [310] 311 [312] 313 [314] 315 [316] 317 [318] 319 [320] 321 [322] 323 [324] 325 [326] 327 [328] 329 [330] 331 [332] 333 [334] 335 [336] 337 [338–40] 341 [342] 343 [344] 345 [346–50] 351 [352] 353 [354–58] 359 [360] 361 [362] 363 [364] 365 [366] 367 [368] 369 [370] 371 [372] 373 [374] 375 [376] 377 [378] 379 [380] 381 [382] 383 [384] 385 [386] 387 [388] 389 [390] 391 [392–94] 395 [396] 397 [398] 399 [400–402] 403 [404] 405 [406] 407 [408–12] 413 [414] 415 [416] 417 [418] 419 [420] 421 [422] 423 [424] 425 [426] 427 [428] 429 [430] 431 [432] 433 [434–36]. Illustrations: [iv–v], [17], 29, [40], [57], 85, [102], [140–41], 149, [209], [240–41], [266], [326], [348–49], [356–57], [393]. Available: 22 October 1976. Published: 6 December 1976. Publication: 25,000 copies of the first printing. Locations: JG, JH, SIU-C. Awarded the National Book Critics Circle Award for Fiction in 1976.

1b New York: Knopf, [October 1976]. Source: publisher's archivist.

1c New York: Knopf, [November 1976]. Source: publisher's archivist.

1d Camp Hill, Pa.: Book-of-the-Month Club, [7 January 1976].

Brown binding; identified with a star blind-stamped on back
binding. Source: publisher's archivist.

1e New York: Knopf, [February 1977]. Source: publisher's archivist.

1f New York: Knopf, [March 1977]. Source: publisher's archivist.

1g Camp Hill, Pa.: Book-of-the-Month Club, [3 March 1977]. Source:
publisher's archivist.

1h New York: Knopf, [March 1977]. Source: publisher's archivist.

1i Camp Hill, Pa.: Book-of-the-Month Club, [18 March 1977].
Source: publisher's archivist.

1j New York: Knopf, [April 1977]. Source: publisher's archivist.

1k New York: Knopf, [April 1977]. Source: publisher's archivist.

1l London: Cape, [21 July 1977]. Without illustrations. Location:
British Museum.

1m An unauthorized photocopy [n.d.]. Location: JH. This photocopy
of the first edition was offered for sale by Chin Shan Books, 89-C
Chung Shan Rd. N. (2), Taipei, Taiwan.

1n Middletown, Pa.: Quality Paperback Book Club, [December
1977]. Wrappers. Source: publisher's archivist.

2a New York: Ballantine, [January 1978]. Wrappers. No. 27193.
Source: Publisher's archivist.

AA.XIX Translations

Luce d'ottobre. Trans. Cristina Bertea. Rome: Editori Riuniti, 1978.
502 pages.

Luz de otoño. Buenos Aires: Emecé Editores, 1978. 417 pages.

John Gardner
October Light

Alfred A. Knopf   A NOVEL

JOHN GARDNER

THE KING OF THE
HUMMINGBIRDS
and Other Tales

Illustrated by Michael Sporn

ALFRED A. KNOPF · NEW YORK

THIS IS A BORZOI BOOK PUBLISHED BY ALFRED A. KNOPF, INC.

Text Copyright © 1977 by Boskydell Artists Ltd. Illustration Copyright © 1977 by Michael Sporn. All rights reserved under International and Pan-American Copyright Conventions. Published in the United States by Alfred A. Knopf, Inc., New York, and simultaneously in Canada by Random House of Canada Limited, Toronto. Distributed by Random House, Inc., New York. Library of Congress Cataloging in Publication Data. Gardner, John Champlin 1933— The king of the hummingbirds, and other tales. SUMMARY: Four fairy tales featuring a stupid coppersmith, a son, a witch unhappy in her profession, a prince with leave to loose things, and a tailor bespectacled Jewish boy who hopes to marry a princess. 1. Fairy tales. [1. Fairy tales] 1. Sporn, Michael, II. Title. PZ8.G226Ki [Fic] 76-42457 ISBN 0-394-83516-0 ISBN 0-394-93516-5 (lib. bdg.) Manufactured in the United States of America 2987654321

A.XX *The King of the Hummingbirds and Other Tales* (1977). Illustrated by
Michael Sporn

1a New York: Knopf. Hard cover, dust wrapper; library binding.
Trim size: 16.1 x 22.7 cm. Collation: [1–3]^{12}. (First and last leaves
are pastedowns.) [i–x] [1–2] 3–6 [7] 8–13 [14] 15–16 [17–18] 19–22
[23] 24–27 [28] 29–30 [31–32] 33–36 [37] 38–41 [42] 43 [44–46] 47–51
[52] 53–56 [57] 58 [59–62]. Illustrations: [ii], [7], [14], [23], [28],
[37], [42], [52], [57]. Contents: "The King of the Hummingbirds"
(see C.20); "The Witch's Wish"; "The Pear Tree" (see C.21); "The
Gnome and the Dragons." Available: 23 January 1977. Published:
2 March 1977. Publication: 13,500 copies of the first printing.
Locations: JG, JH, SIU-C.
1b New York: Knopf, [September 1977]. Source: publisher's archivist.
1c Camp Hill, Pa.: Book-of-the-Month Club, [September 1977].
Source: publisher's archivist. A Juvenile Dividend offered as part
of a three-volume set with *Dragon, Dragon and Other Tales* and
Gudgekin the Thistle Girl and Other Tales.
1d Camp Hill, Pa.: Book-of-the-Month Club, [December 1977].
Source: publisher's archivist. A Juvenile Dividend offered as part
of a three-volume set with *Dragon, Dragon and Other Tales* and
Gudgekin the Thistle Girl and Other Tales.
2a New York: Bantam, [February 1979]. Wrappers. Bantam Skylark.
No. 83319-8. Location: JH.

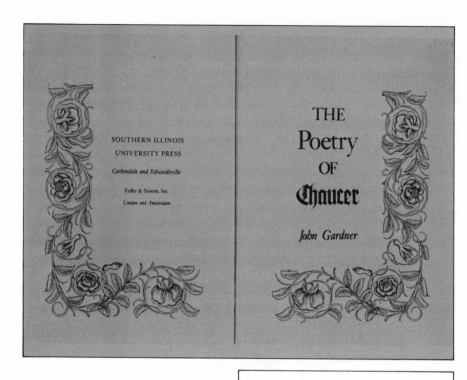

SOUTHERN ILLINOIS
UNIVERSITY PRESS

Carbondale and Edwardsville

Feffer & Simons, Inc.
London and Amsterdam

THE
Poetry
OF
Chaucer

John Gardner

Library of Congress Cataloging in Publication Data

Gardner, John Champlin, 1933–
  The poetry of Chaucer.

  Includes bibliographical references and index.
  1. Chaucer, Geoffrey, d. 1400—Criticism and
interpretation. I. Title.
PR1924.G3   821'.1   76-22713
ISBN 0-8093-0772-3

A.XXI *The Poetry of Chaucer* (1977)

1a Carbondale and Edwardsville: Southern Illinois University Press; London and Amsterdam; Feffer & Simons. Hard cover, dust wrapper. Trim size: 15.6 x 23.7 cm. Collation: [1–14]¹⁶. [i–vi] vii–xiii [xiv] xv–xxxv [xxxvi–xxxviii] 1–337 [338–40] 341–408 [409–10]. Available: 3 January 1977. Published: 28 March 1977. Publication: 1,819 copies of the first printing. Locations: JH, SIU-C.

1b Carbondale and Edwardsville: Southern Illinois University; London and Amsterdam: Feffer & Simons, [July 1977]. Source: publisher's archivist.

1c Carbondale and Edwardsville: Southern Illinois University; London and Amsterdam: Feffer & Simons, [October 1978]. Wrappers. Location: JH. This offset printing was reduced in size.

1d Carbondale and Edwardsville: Southern Illinois University; London and Amsterdam: Feffer & Simons, [December 1978]. Wrappers. Source: publisher's archivist.

The Life & Times of Chaucer

by

John Gardner

ornaments by

J. Wolf

Alfred A. Knopf   New York, 1977

THIS IS A BORZOI BOOK
PUBLISHED BY ALFRED A. KNOPF, INC.

Copyright © 1977 by John Gardner
All rights reserved under International
and Pan-American Copyright Conventions.
Published in the United States
by Alfred A. Knopf, Inc., New York,
and simultaneously in Canada
by Random House of Canada Limited, Toronto.

Library of Congress Cataloging in Publication Data
Gardner, John Champlin, (Date)
The life and times of Chaucer.

Includes bibliographical references and index.
1. Chaucer, Geoffrey, d. 1400—Biography.   I.   Title.
PR1905.G3   821'.1 [B]   76-1915
ISBN 0-394-49317-6

Distributed by Random House, Inc., New York.
Manufactured in the United States of America
First Edition

A.XXII *The Life and Times of Chaucer* (1977). Illustrated by J. Wolf

1a New York: Knopf. Hard cover, dust wrapper. Trim size: 15.6 x 23.6 cm. Collation: [1–11]^{16}. (The first leaf is pasted to free endpaper.) [i–vi] vii–ix [x] [1–2] 3–56 [57–58] 59–84 [85–86] 87–317 [318] 319–28 i–x [xi–xii]. Inset illustrations at chapter openings: 3, 21, 52, 90, 127, 168, 204, 228, 263, 286, 315. Full-page illustrations: [57], [85]. Available: 5 February 1977. Published: 5 April 1977. Publication: 10,000 copies of the first printing. Locations: JH, SIU-C.

1b New York: Knopf, [May 1977]. Source: publisher's archivist.

1c New York: Reader's Subscription, [May 1977]. Source: publisher's archivist. No distinguishing marks; printed and bound with Knopf's copies.

1d Camp Hill, Pa.: Book-of-the-Month Club, [1 June 1977]. Source: publisher's archivist. Dark red binding; identified with a square blind-stamped on back binding.

1e Middletown, Pa.: Quality Paperback Book Club, [June 1977]. Wrappers. Source: publisher's archivist.

1f New York: Knopf, [July 1977]. Source: publisher's archivist.

1g New York: Knopf, [July 1977]. Source: publisher's archivist.

1h Camp Hill, Pa.: Book-of-the-Month Club, [August 1977]. Source: publisher's archivist.

1i Camp Hill, Pa.: Book-of-the-Month Club, [September 1977]. Source: Publisher's archivist.

1j London: Cape, [17 November 1977]. Source: publisher's archivist. This printing was produced for Cape by Knopf.

1k Camp Hill, Pa.: [February 1978]. Source: publisher's archivist.

1l Middletown, Pa.: Quality Paperback Book Club, [June 1977]. Wrappers. Source: publisher's archivist.

1m New York: Vintage, [21 April 1978]. Wrappers. No. V-500. Location: JH. This offset printing was reduced in size.

1n Camp Hill, Pa.: Book-of-the Month Club, [September 1977]. Source: publisher's archivist.

1o Camp Hill, Pa.: Book-of-the-Month Club, [May 1979]. Source: publisher's archivist.

Forthcoming

London: Paladin Books, [Spring 1979–Spring 1980]. Source: Cape archivist.

A Child's
BESTIARY
BY
JOHN GARDNER

with additional poems by
Lucy Gardner &
Eugene Rudzewicz
&

drawings by
Lucy, Joel, Joan
& John Gardner

Alfred A. Knopf / New York

THIS IS A BORZOI BOOK PUBLISHED BY ALFRED A. KNOPF, INC.

Copyright © 1977 by Boskydell Artists Ltd. All rights reserved
under International and Pan-American Copyright Conventions.
Published in the United States by Alfred A. Knopf, Inc., New
York, and simultaneously in Canada by Random House of Canada
Limited, Toronto. Distributed by Random House, Inc., New York.

Library of Congress Cataloging in Publication Data
Gardner, John Champlin, 1933– A child's bestiary.
Summary: A collection of humorous verses about animals,
friendly or otherwise. 1. Animals–Poetry. [1. Animals–Poetry]
I. Title. PS3557.A712C5 811'.5'4 77-3945 ISBN 0-394-83483-6
ISBN 0-394-93483-0 Manufactured in the United States of
America

A.XXIII *A Child's Bestiary* (1977). By John Gardner/with Additional Poems by/Lucy Gardner &/Eugene Rudzewicz/&/Drawings by/Lucy, Joel, Joan/& John Gardner

1a New York: Knopf. Hard cover, dust wrapper; library binding. Trim size: 16.1 x 22.8 cm. Collation: [1–4]¹². (First and last leaves are pastedowns.) [i–xviii] [l] 2–18 [19] 20–25 [26] 27–69 [70–78]. Illustrations: [xvi], 2–12, 14–16, [19]–[26], 29–30, 32–33, 35–60, 63, 65–68. Photograph: Gardner and collaborators [71]. Contents: See "The Beasts" ([10–11]) for a list of the 68 beasts, real and imaginary. Available: 21 July 1977. Published: October 1977. Publication: 12,500 copies of the first printing. The poem entitled "The Crow" was reprinted separately (with an autobiographical statement) on a folded sheet; see A.XXIV.

Department of English presents

THE WRITERS FORUM

STATE UNIVERSITY OF NEW YORK
COLLEGE AT BROCKPORT

FALL, 1977

A.XXIV *The Crow* (1977). Cover Graphic by Robin Roy Rubin

Brockport, New York: The Writers Forum. Copyright: Fall [October] 1977. Folded sheet. Blue paper. Trim size: 21.7 x 28.1 cm. Collation: single sheet folded once, 4 pp: [1] title page; [2] autobiographical statement by Gardner, with photograph; [3] "The Crow"; [4] history and schedule of The Writers Forum. Publication: approximately 450 copies were printed for Gardner's reading at the State University of New York College at Brockport on 5 October 1977. Location: JH. The poem was reprinted from *A Child's Bestiary*, published that same month (although available 21 July 1977).

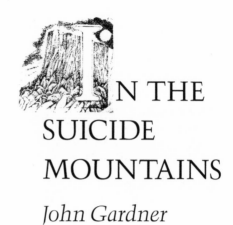

N THE
SUICIDE
MOUNTAINS

John Gardner

Alfred A. Knopf   New York   1977

THIS IS A BORZOI BOOK PUBLISHED BY ALFRED A. KNOPF, INC.

Copyright © 1977 by Boskydell Artists, Ltd.
All rights reserved under International and Pan-American
Copyright Conventions. Published in the United States by
Alfred A. Knopf, Inc., New York, and simultaneously in Canada
by Random House of Canada Limited, Toronto. Distributed
by Random House, Inc., New York.

The abbot's tales and the baby's tale are adapted from
traditional Russian fairy tales as collected by
Aleksandr Afanas'ev, translated by Norbert Guterman.

Library of Congress Cataloging in Publication Data
Gardner, John Champlin [date]
In the suicide mountains.
I. Title.
PZ4.G23117In3   [PS3557.A712]   813'.5'4   77-74993
ISBN 0-394-41880-8
Manufactured in the United States of America
First Edition

A.XXV *In the Suicide Mountains* (1977). Illustrated by Joe Servello

1a New York: Knopf. Hard cover, dust wrapper. Trim size: 19.0 x
    21.1 cm. Collation: [1–4]¹⁶ [5]⁸ [6]¹⁶. [i–xii] [1–4] 5 [6–8] 9 [10] 11
    [12–16] 17 [18–20] 21 [22] 23 [24] 25 [26–28] 29 [30–32] 33 [34–36] 37
    [38–40] 41 [42] 43 [44–46] 47 [48] 49 [50] 51 [52–54] 55 [56–60] 61 [62]
    63 [64] 65 [66–70] 71 [72] 73 [74] 75 [76] 77 [78–80] 81 [82] 83 [84] 85
    [86] 87 [88–90] 91 [92–96] 97 [98–102] 103 [104] 105 [106] 107 [108]
    109 [110] 111 [112–16] 117 [118–20] 121 [122–24] 125 [126] 127
    [128–32] 133 [134–36] 137 [138] 139 [140–42] 143 [144–48] 149
    [150–52] 153 [154] 155 [156–64]. Inset illustrations at chapter
    openings: [3], [13], [19], [31], [38], [45], [57], [67], [79], [93], [99],
    [106], [119], [129], [135], [147], [157]. Full-page illustrations: [vii],
    [7], [15], [27], [35], [39], [53], [59], [69], [89], [95], [101], [114–15],
    [123], [131], [141], [145], [151], [159]. Available: 23 September
    1977. Published: 20 October 1977. Publication: 17,500 copies of the
    first printing. Locations: JH, SIU-C. The uncorrected galleys sent
    to reviewers contained sample illustrations.
1b New York: Knopf, [November 1977]. Source: publisher's ar-
    chivist.

ON
MORAL
FICTION

ᴸᴸᴸᴸᴸᴸᴸᴸᴸᴸᴸᴸᴸᴸᴸᴸᴸᴸᴸᴸᴸᴸᴸ

JOHN GARDNER

Basic Books, Inc., Publishers

NEW YORK

A portion of this book appeared, in different form, in "Death by Art: 'Some Men Kill You with a Six-gun, Some Men with a Pen,' " in *Critical Inquiry*, vol. 3, no. 4 (1977). Copyright © 1977 by The University of Chicago. All rights reserved. Reprinted by permission of The University of Chicago Press.

Library of Congress Cataloging in Publication Data

Gardner, John Champlin, 1933-
  On moral fiction.

Includes bibliographical references.
  1. Literature and morals. 2. Arts and morals.
I. Title.
PN49.G345   801   77-20409
ISBN: 0-465-05225-8

A.XXVI *On Moral Fiction* (1978)

1a New York: Basic Books. Hard cover, dust wrapper. Trim size: 13.6 x 20.7 cm. Collation: [1–7]¹⁶. [i–viii] [1–2] 3–101 [102–4] 105–205 [206] 207–14 [215–16]. Available: 3 March 1978. Published: 19 April 1978. Publication: 7,000 copies of the first printing. Locations: JH, SIU-C. Sections of this book incorporate essays that appeared in *Hudson Review* (see E.20); *Western Humanities Review* (see E.22); and *Critical Inquiry* (see E.23). A brief excerpt appears in *Saturday Review* (see E.26).
1b New York: Basic Books, [September 1979]. Wrappers. No. CN 5048. Source: publisher's archivist.

Nicholas Vergette 1923-1974

For some time, not all by delusion,
we spoke of the world as meaningless and scant;
observed the decay of old notions, the strange, worldwide
    decline
like ailing light in a universe grown old, beginning
to wander from the point. Conversation would dim
and we'd sink out of thought for a moment, gaze down
at a gray gin and tonic like the crystal ball
with nothing to report.
And he, this man, was one of us in that as in everything.

Life is perhaps not much, considered objectively.
Considered, that is, by a man all alone in his living room,
staring at the embers in his fireplace, as he occasionally
    did.
Plans fail, fools squabble over trifles, the tawdry and dull
    prevails,
or so it seemed even to him, from time to time, as to all
    of us.
But his house was strong with his work—collages and
    paintings, clay pots—
and the night outside his window was alive with his
    sculptures, his trees,
his althea, hollyhocks, ceramic tables—beyond those the
    hedges,
the horse trails and jumps that gave shape to his farm,
his own hands' labor—so that when he at last looked up
    he saw
the darkness bending down to him, attendant to his will.

He doubted the old stiff-minded gods, as do all of us,
disliked the unduly religious for their cowardice, their
    murder of the woods;
yet all he spoke or cast was mysterious and holy, and
    meant to be—
as quick with the spirit of God as sunlit pastures, or
    morning
hurrying to rise before Vergette, who came
like an old-time Greek to cut wood, plant flowers,
prepare the world for his son, and with songs
like "Ragtime Cowboy Joe" prepare
his son for a world not meaningless, not scant.

He put his faith in his hands, and in his students' hands,
flooring the ancient abyss with art till he forgot it was
    there.
His faith was in his friends,
in vast, good humanity excluding not even that old rascal
    Chumly
who married a gorilla.
"A girl gorilla. Nothing queer about old Chumly!"
His faith was in stones, and in his own bright mottled
    imitations of stones,
in bronze, wood, plastic; in towering forms, in squat
    forms, in walls,
whatever his artist's eye might seize and his heart
    approve. So—slowly—
the world took shape, and we began to understand
the shape was there from the beginning.

Then he died, as his work should have taught us to
    predict.
The dogs howled. It rained. We should have expected it.
He became once more like the clay he himself had
    fashioned or discarded
as need or the crying wind demanded. Rightly, or anyway
    submissively.
Beneath the wall he'd built, with the blind human face
    looking south,
he'd planted a penny—obedient to custom Stonehenges
    old,
not in propitiation of the gods but in admission of their
    power,
the stately progression of flowers and ice. The floor he
    built
and came to believe in so fully he dared us to dance on
    its stones
we test now with tentative steps. It will hold.

"Nothing's alone," he told me once. "When I start up
    my lawn mower
the grass cries out in anguish. Think of it!"
And I saw what he saw: the grass and ourselves and the
    stars one work.
Saw it, or glimpsed it for an instant, and then felt unsure
    again.
So now I cry out like the grass, like all of us,
sick with memories of things once filled with light, and
    say
to whatever gods he prayed to with his hands,
worshipped with his wheel—the tongs and knives of his
    firing and carving—
The best of monuments has vanished. Take it in.

This broadside was printed during the summer of 1978
to coincide with the Lord John Press publication
of *Poems.* Limited to one-hundred and fifty copies.

A.XXVII *Nicholas Vergette 1923–1974* (1978)

Northridge, California: Lord John Press. Copyright: 18 September 1978. Broadside. Trim size: 31.5 x 45.0 cm. Publication: 150 copies "printed during the summer of 1978 to coincide with the Lord John Press publication of *Poems*." Location: JH. This poem was first read by Gardner at the memorial service held for Nicholas Vergette in Carbondale, Illinois, 28 February 1974. It was printed earlier in *Nicholas Vergette* (see B.15) and *Craft Horizons* (see D.17); and later in *Poems*.

Poems

John Gardner

Lord John Press
Northridge, California
1978

A.XXVIII *Poems* (1978)

1a Northridge, California: Lord John Press. Hard cover: clothbound and leather-bound; no dust wrapper. Trim size: 15.0 x 23.0 cm. Collation: [1–7]^8 [8]^6. [i–viii] ix–x [xi–xii] 1–25 [26–28] 29–85 [86–88] 89–108 [109–12]. Contents: Preface. Part I: "Song"; "Bon Voyage" (see D.8); "Frankenstein" (see D.9); "The Judge Goes Riding"; "The Motorcycle Riders" (see A.XVII, D.14); "Legend" (see D.15); "Setting for an Old Welsh Line" (see D.13); "Lenten Is Come with Love: An Imitation" (see D.12); "Song"; "Art, Life, and Aunt Etwell" (see D.3); "The Visitor"; "Dream Vision"; "Guest Preacher"; "To the Coven"; "Nicholas Vergette 1923–1974" (see A.XXVII, B.15, D.17). Part II: "Putcha Putcha"; "The Love Poet"; "Los Angeles" (see D.16); "Desire on Sunday Morning" (see D.11); "To a Cloud"; "To a Lady"; "Song in an Old Time Style"; "Song of the Jubilant Hero"; "Lyric"; "Pictures from an Old Album" (see D.5); "Five Sonnets for Joan"; "Yvain"; "The Ruptured Goat" (see D.4); "She Loves Me Not"; "The Drunken Swimmers"; "The Astronaut in the Rose Garden"; "The Stranger in the Grove" (see D.7); "History Lesson"; "Literature"; "The Witch of the Imagination"; "In the Garden"; "The Governor in the Dark" (see D.6). Part III: "Collisions"; "Persimmons" (see D.10). Available: 10 November 1978. Published: 10 November 1978. Publication: limited signed edition: 300 numbered copies (clothbound); 26 lettered copies (leather-bound); 15 presentation copies (clothbound). Location: JH.

John Gardner

RUMPELSTILTSKIN

NEW LONDON PRESS   /   Dallas

ISBN 0-89683-012-8
ISBN 0-89683-011-X (limited edition)
Manufactured in the United States

A.XXIX *Rumpelstiltskin* (1978)

1a Dallas: New London Press. Wrappers: self-covered prepublication performance copy. Trim size: 13.6 x 21.2 cm. Collation: 32 leaves, stapled twice at center. [1–4] [i]–ii [1–3] 4–56 [57–58]. Contents: Preface by Gardner, and libretto. Available: December 1978. Published: 26 December 1978. Publication: 1,000 copies printed for sale at performances in Philadelphia by The Opera Company of Philadelphia, 26–30 December 1978. According to Gardner, approximately 25 of the copies were signed, prior to sale, by him and Joseph Baber, the composer. Location: JH.
1b Dallas: New London Press, [30 September 1979]. Copyright page: "FIRST PRINTING." Hard cover, no dust wrapper. Publication: limited signed edition: 250 copies; lettered edition: 26 copies; unsigned trade edition: 750 copies. Location: JH.

John Gardner

FRANKENSTEIN

NEW LONDON PRESS / Dallas

FIRST PRINTING

Copyright © 1979 by John Gardner
All right reserved.
Manufactured in the United States of America

ISBN 0-89683-010-1
ISBN 0-89683-009-8 (limited edition)

A.XXX *Frankenstein* (1979)

1a   Dallas: New London Press. Hard cover, no dust wrapper. Trim size: 13.6 x 21.2 cm. Collation: [1–5]⁸. [π1–π4] [i] ii–iii [iv] [1] 2–67 [68–72]. Contents: Preface by Gardner, and libretto. Available: 10 August 1979. Published: 30 September 1979. Publication: limited signed edition: 250 copies; lettered edition: 26 copies; unsigned trade edition: 750 copies. Location: JH. This opera has not yet had a full-scale production.

WILLIAM WILSON

John Gardner

NEW LONDON PRESS
Dallas, Texas

FIRST PRINTING

ISBN 0-89683-008-X
ISBN 0-89683-007-1 (limited edition)

A.XXXI *William Wilson* (1979)

1a   Dallas: New London Press. Hard cover, no dust wrapper. Trim size: 13.6 x 21.2 cm. Collation: [1–3]⁸ [4]⁴ [5–6]⁸. [π1–π4] [i] ii–v [vi] [1–3] 4–72 [73–78]. Contents: Preface by Gardner, and libretto. Available: 10 August 1979. Published: 30 September 1979. Publication: limited signed edition: 250 copies; lettered edition: 26 copies; unsigned trade edition: 750 copies. Location: JH. This opera has not yet been produced.

Forthcoming

John Gardner: An Interview. Dallas: New London Press, [October 1979].

Vlemk: The Box-Painter. Tale. Northridge, California: Lord John Press, [November 1979].

Death and the Maiden. Play. Dallas: New London Press, [January 1980].

The Temptation Game. Radio play. Dallas: New London Press, [January 1980].

Freddy's Book. Two novellas. New York: Knopf, [March 1980].

Projected

One-volume selection from past numbers of *MSS.* Dallas: New London Press, [1980].

"The Angel." Radio play. Dallas: New London Press, [1980].

"Samson and the Witch." Libretto. Dallas: New London Press, [1980].

"The Water Horse." Radio play. Dallas: New London Press, [1980].

One-volume collection of three radio plays ("The Angel," "The Temptation Game," and "The Water Horse"). Dallas: New London Press, [1980].

"Helen at Home." Play. Dallas: New London Press, [1981].

"The Latest Word from Delphi." Play. Dallas: New London Press, [1981].

"The Pied Piper of Hamlin." Libretto. Dallas: New London Press, [1981].

B. First-Appearance Contributions to Books, Pamphlets, and Portfolios

Titles in which material by Gardner appears for the first time in a book, pamphlet, or portfolio, arranged chronologically. Previously unpublished items are so identified.

B.1 Rev. of *Art and Tradition in Sir Gawain and the Green Knight*, by Larry D. Benson. *Critical Studies of Sir Gawain and the Green Knight*. Ed. Donald Roy Howard and Christian Zacher. Notre Dame, Ind.: University of Notre Dame Press, 1968, pp. 307–10. Reprinted from *Journal of English and Germanic Philology*; see F.1.

B.2 Foreword to *The Construction of "Paradise Lost,"* by Burton Jasper Weber. Carbondale and Edwardsville: Southern Illinois University Press; London and Amsterdam: Feffer & Simons, 1971, p. ix. Gardner is general editor of this and other studies in the Literary Structures series.

B.3 "The Temptation of St. Ivo." In *The Secret Life of Our Times: New Fiction from "Esquire."* Ed. Gordon Lish. New York: Doubleday, 1973, pp. 435–47. An excerpt; restored to full length in *The King's Indian*; see C.12.

B.4 "The Song of Grendel." In *The Secret Life of Our Times: New Fiction from "Esquire."* Ed. Gordon Lish. New York: Doubleday, 1973, pp. 489–520. Reprints an excerpt from chaps. 1–4, and 6 of *Grendel*, excluding original illustrations; see C.8.

B.5 Foreword to *Forms of Glory: Structure and Sense in Virgil's "Aeneid,"* by J. William Hunt. Carbondale and Edwardsville: Southern Illinois University Press; London and Amsterdam: Feffer & Simons, Inc., 1973, pp. ix–[x]. Gardner is general editor of this and other studies in the Literary Structures series.

B.6 Introduction to *Grendel*. Trans. René Daillie. Paris: Denoël, 1974, pp. 19–23. In French; see AA.VIII.

B.7 "John Napper Sailing through the Universe." In *Modern Occasions 2 New Fiction, Criticism, Poetry*. Ed. Philip Rahv. Port Washington, N.Y.: Kennikat, 1974, pp. 213–27. Reprinted in *The King's Indian*.

B.8   Introduction sheet for *The Sunlight Dialogues, Original Litho-
        graphs by John Napper. An Additional Set of Illustrations to the
        Novel by John Gardner*. New York: Larcada Editions, 1972. This
        portfolio, with prospectus, was published in an edition of one
        hundred sets of thirteen lithographs, signed and numbered. See
        H.18 for abstract of Gardner's comment on Napper's illustra-
        tions.

B.9   "The Things." In *Prize Stories 1974: The O. Henry Awards*. Ed.
        William Abrahams. Garden City, N.Y.: Doubleday, 1974, pp.
        105–16. Reprinted from *Perspective*, with an "s" restored to the
        misprinted title, "The Thing"; see C.10.

B.10   Foreword to *Wedges and Wings: The Patterning of "Paradise
        Regained,"* by Burton Jasper Weber. Carbondale and Ed-
        wardsville: Southern Illinois University Press; Feffer & Simons,
        Inc., 1974 pp. ix–x. Gardner is general editor of this and other
        studies in the Literary Structures series.

B.11   "John Gardner." In *The New Fiction: Interviews with Innovative
        American Writers*. Ed. Joe David Bellamy. Urbana, Chicago,
        London: University of Illinois Press, 1974, pp. 169–93. Inter-
        viewed by Joe David Bellamy and Pat Ensworth; reprinted from
        Fiction International; see H.23.

B.12   "John Gardner: A Profile." In *The Writer in American Society*.
        Washington: United States Information Service, [1974], pp.
        6–11. Comments by Gardner and three photographs; published
        in Japanese for USIS tour of Japan (8 September–5 October
        1974).

B.13   "The Way We Write Now." In *The Writer in American Society*.
        Washington: United States Information Service, [1974], pp.
        12–17. Translated into Japanese from *New York Times Book
        Review*; see E.14.

B.14   *Writers on Writing*. Rochester: University of Rochester, [1974].
        An eight-page pamphlet that transcribes a panel discussion on
        WXXI-TV involving Gardner, Judith Rascoe, and George P.
        Elliott, with L. J. Davis as moderator. Taped at WXXI-TV,
        Rochester, 9 July 1973; used as a promotional for The Writers
        Workshop, in 1974; for abstract see H.15.

B.15   "Poem in Memory of Nick Vergette." In *Nicholas Vergette*. Ed.
        Robert A. Walsh. Mount Vernon, Ill.: The Mitchell Museum, [20
        April 1974], [p. xxv]. This poem was first read by Gardner at the
        memorial service for Nicholas Vergette held in Carbondale,
        Illinois, 28 February 1974. Reprinted under different titles in

Craft Horizons (see D.17); as a broadside (see A.XXVII); and in *Poems*.

B.16 "Guilt and the World's Complexity: The Murder of Ongentheow and the Slaying of the Dragon." In *Anglo-Saxon Poetry: Essays in Appreciation*. Ed. Lewis E. Nicholson and Dolores Warwick Frese. Notre Dame, Ind.: University of Notre Dame Press, 1975, pp. 14–22. *Festschrift* volume for Professor John C. McGalliard.

B.17 "Queen Louisa." In *Superfiction, or The American Story Transformed: An Anthology*. Ed. Joe David Bellamy. New York: Vintage, 1975, pp. 157–72. Reprinted from *The King's Indian*.

B.18 Afterword to *The Red Napoleon*, by Floyd Gibbons. Carbondale and Edwardsville: Southern Illinois University Press; London and Amsterdam: Feffer & Simons, Inc., 1976, pp. 477–86. New York: Popular Library, 1977, pp. 375–84. Wrappers. See K.450.

B.19 "Conversations with John Gardner on Writers and Writing." In *Authors in the News*. Detroit: Gale Research Co., 1976, pp. 168–69. Reprinted from *Detroit Magazine*; see H.32.

B.20 Preface to *Music from Home: Selected Poems*, by Colleen J. McElroy. Carbondale and Edwardsville: Southern Illinois University Press, London and Amsterdam: Feffer & Simons, Inc., 1976, pp. ix–xi. Gardner is general editor of this work in the Sagittarius Poetry series.

B.21 *Self-Portrait: Book People Picture Themselves*. Ed. Burt Britton, New York: Random House, 1976, p. 32. Gardner's self-portrait is a cartoon signed "John Gardner April 8, 1974"; for further details, see H.50.

B.22 "Southern Illinois University Press." *Pages*, Vol. I. Detroit: Gale Research, 1976, pp. 182–87.

B.23 "Moral Fiction." In *The Pushcart Prize, III: Best of the Small Presses (1978–1979 Edition)*. Ed. Bill Henderson et al. Yonkers, N.Y.: Pushcart Press, 1978, pp. 52–68. Reprinted in *On Moral Fiction*.

B.24 Foreword to *Homer's "Iliad": The Shield of Memory*, by Kenneth John Atchity. Carbondale and Edwardsville: Southern Illinois University Press; London and Amsterdam: Feffer & Simons, Inc., 1978, pp. ix–x. Gardner is general editor of this and other studies in the Literary Structures series.

B.25 Foreword to *Kingship and Common Profit in Gower's "Confessio Amantis,"* by Russell A. Peck. Carbondale and Edwardsville:

Southern Illinois University Press; London and Amsterdam: Feffer & Simons, Inc., 1978, pp. ix–x. Gardner is general editor of this and other studies in the Literary Structures series.

B.26 "John Gardner." In *Conversations with Writers*, Vol. I. Detroit: Gale Research, 1978, pp. 82–103. Interviewed in June 1977 by C. E. Frazer Clark, Jr.; see H.86.

B.27 "Redemption." In *The Best American Short Stories 1978*. Ed. Ted Solotaroff with Shannon Ravenel. Boston: Houghton Mifflin, 1978, pp. 248–61. Reprinted from *Atlantic Monthly*; see C.23.

B.28 Foreword to *Flamboyant Drama: A Study of "The Castle of Perseverance," "Mankind," and "Wisdom,"* by Michael R. Kelley. Carbondale and Edwardsville: Southern Illinois University Press; London and Amsterdam: Feffer & Simons, 1979, pp. ix–x. Gardner is general editor of this and other studies in the Literary Structures series.

C. Fiction in Magazines and Newspapers

First publication in magazines and newspapers of fiction by Gardner, arranged chronologically. All reprintings and significant revisions are noted.

C.1 "Freshman." *Boulder* [DePauw], 15 (February 1952), 1, 20. Gardner is listed as a member of the editorial staff.

C.2 "Nickel Mountain." *Reflections: Washington University Student Review*, No. 4 (1955), pp. 42–56. Revised for *Nickel Mountain;* Gardner is listed as a member of the editorial staff.

C.3 "A Little Night Music." *Northwest Review*, 4 (Spring 1961), 30–40. Revised for *The Sunlight Dialogues.*

C.4 "The Edge of the Woods." *Quarterly Review of Literature*, 11, No. 3 (1963), 268–301. Revised for *Nickel Mountain.*

C.5 "Nickel Mountain." *Southern Review*, NS 1 (Spring 1966), 374–418. Revised for *Nickel Mountain.*

C.6 "The Spike in the Door." *Ball State University Forum*, 8 (Autumn 1967), 52–55. Revised for *Nickel Mountain.*

C.7 "The Grave." *Quarterly Review of Literature*, 17, Nos. 3–4 (1971), 354–71. Revised for *Nickel Mountain.*

C.8 "The Song of Grendel." *Esquire*, 76 (October 1971), 138–39, 180–96. An excerpt from chaps. 1–4, and 6 of *Grendel*, excluding original illustrations; reprinted in *The Secret Life of Our Times;* see B.4.

C.9 "The Darkening Green." *Iowa Review*, 3 (Winter 1972, 46–48.

C.10 "The Thing." *Perspective*, 17 (Winter 1972), 17–27. See *Nickel Mountain* and *Prize Stories 1974* (B.9), where an "s" is restored to the misprinted title.

C.11 "Pastoral Care." *Audience*, 2 (May–June 1972), 24–39. Illus. James McMullan. Reprinted in *The King's Indian.*

C.12 "The Temptation of St. Ivo." *Esquire*, 78 (July 1972), 133–35, 164–69. An excerpt: reprinted in *The Secret Life of Our Times* (see B.3); restored to full length in *The King's Indian.*

C.13 "The Ravages of Spring." *Fantastic Science Fiction and Fantasy*

Stories, 22 (April 1973), 46–63, 121. Reprinted in *The King's Indian.*

C.14 "Nickel Mountain." *Redbook,* 142 (November 1973), 153–75. A condensation of *Nickel Mountain.*

C.15 "The Music Lover." *Antaeus: Special Fiction Issue.* Ed. Daniel Halpern, Nos. 13–14 (Spring–Summer 1974), 176–82.

C.16 "King Gregor and the Fool." *Atlantic Monthly,* 233 (May 1974), 61–66. Reprinted in *The King's Indian.*

C.17 "The Joy of the Just." *American Poetry Review,* 3 (July–August 1974), 12–18.

C.18 "John Gardner's *Grendel." Literary Cavalcade,* 27 (November 1974), 4–9. Reprints chap. 6 of *Grendel* in the heavily edited *Esquire* version (see C.8), but uses nine of the original illustrations.

C.19 "The Warden." *Tri-Quarterly,* 29 (Winter 1974), 5–39. Reprinted in *The King's Indian.*

C.20 "King of the Hummingbirds." *Saturday Evening Post,* 248 (April 1976), 49–51, 108. Reprinted in *The King of the Hummingbirds.*

C.21 "The Pear Tree." *Saturday Evening Post,* 248 (October 1976), 18–20. Reprinted in *The King of the Hummingbirds.*

C.22 "Trumpeter." *Esquire,* 86 (December 1976), 114–16, 182.

C.23 "Redemption." *Atlantic Monthly,* 239 (May 1977), 48–50, 55–56, 58–59. Reprinted in *The Best American Stories 1978;* see B.27.

C.24 "Best Seller." *Holiday Inn Companion,* 3 (June 1977), 19–24. Excerpt from *October Light,* pp. 231–37.

C.25 "Stillness." *Hudson Review,* 30 (Winter 1977–78), 549–59.

C.26 "The Library Horror." *Seattle Review,* 2 (Spring 1979), 7–14.

C.27 "Nimram." *Atlantic Monthly,* 244 (September 1979), 39–48. Originally entitled "Amarand"; see H.93.

D. Poetry in Magazines and Newspapers

First publication in magazines and newspapers of poetry by Gardner, arranged chronologically. All reprintings are noted.

D.1 "Mr. Richard Babley's Memorial." *Reflections: Washington University Student Review,* No. 3 (1954), pp. 9–10. Gardner is listed as a member of the editorial staff.

D.2 "The Human Hand." *Reflections: Washington University Student Review,* No. 3 (1954), pp. 11–13. Gardner is listed as a member of the editorial staff.

D.3 "Art, Life, and Aunt Etwell." *Perspective,* 14 (Spring 1965), 40–41. Reprinted in *Poems.*

D.4 "The Ruptured Goat." *Southern Review,* NS 4 (Winter 1968), 162–64. Reprinted in *Poems.*

D.5 "Pictures from an Old Album." *Grassroots* [Southern Illinois University at Carbondale], 1, No. 1 [1968], 10. Reprinted in *Poems.*

D.6 "The Governor in the Dark." *Perspective,* 16 (Winter–Spring 1969), 24–26. Reprinted in *Poems.*

D.7 "The Stranger in the Grove." *Perspective,* 16 (Winter–Spring 1969), 21–23. Reprinted in *Poems.*

D.8 "Bon Voyage." *Kenyon Review,* 31, No. 4 (1969), 504–5. Reprinted in *Poems.*

D.9 "Frankenstein." *Kenyon Review,* 31, No. 4 (1969), 505–6. Reprinted in *Poems.*

D.10 "Persimmons." *Western Humanities Review,* 23 (Spring 1969), 155–57. Reprinted in *Poems.*

D.11 "Desire on Sunday Morning." *Hudson Review,* 23 (Spring 1970), 28–34. Reprinted in *Poems.*

D.12 "Lenten Is Come with Love: An Imitation." *Hudson Review,* 23 (Spring 1970), 34–35. Reprinted in *Poems.*

D.13 "Setting for an Old Welsh Line." *Hudson Review,* 23 (Spring 1970), 35–36. Reprinted in *Poems.*

D.14 "The Motorcycle Riders." *Perspective,* 16 (Autumn 1971), 252.

An enlarged facsimile of a holograph of this poem was published as *A Folger Poetry Broadside;* see A.XVII. Reprinted in *Poems.*

D.15 "Legend." *Perspective,* 16 (Autumn 1971), 251. Reprinted in *Poems.*

D.16 "Los Angeles." *Perspective,* 16 (Autumn 1971), 253. Reprinted in *Poems.*

D.17 "Nicholas Vergette 1923–1974." *Craft Horizons,* 34 (April 1974), 7. This poem was first read by Gardner at the memorial service held for Nicholas Vergette in Carbondale, Illinois, 28 February 1974. It was later reprinted in *Nicholas Vergette* (see B.15); as a broadside (see A.XXVII); and in *Poems.*

D.18 "Lemnos." *Fiction Midwest,* I. No. 1 [Spring 1973], [6–8]. The editors cite "Lemnos" as an excerpt "from the novel *Jason and Medeia* to be published by Alfred A. Knopf in June, 1973." *Jason and Medeia* is, of course, an epic poem.

E. Articles and Essays in Magazines and Newspapers

First publication in magazines and newspapers of articles and essays by Gardner, arranged chronologically.

E.1 *"Bartleby:* Art and Social Commitment." *Philological Quarterly,* 43 (January 1964), 87–98.

E.2 "Theme and Irony in The Wakefield *Mactacio Abel." PMLA,* 80 (December 1965), 515–21.

E.3 *"The Owl and the Nightingale:* A Burlesque." *Papers on Language and Literature,* 2 (Winter 1966), 3–12.

E.4 "The Canon Yeoman's Prologue and Tale: An Interpretation." *Philological Quarterly,* 46 (January 1967), 1–17.

E.5 "Structure and Tone in the *Second Shepherd's Play." Educational Theatre Journal,* 19 (March 1967), 1–8.

E.6 "Introduction." *Papers on the Art and Age of Geoffrey Chaucer, Papers on Language and Literature,* 3 (Supplement, Summer 1967), 1–2. Gardner was a guest editor. See K.451, 452.

E.7 "The Case Against the 'Bradshaw Shift'; or, the Mystery of the Manuscript in the Trunk." *Papers on Language and Literature,* 3 (Summer 1967), 80–106.

E.8 "Imagery and Allusion in The Wakefield Noah Play." *Papers on Language and Literature,* 4 (Winter 1968), 3–12.

E.9 "The Two Prologues to the *Legend of Good Women." Journal of English and Germanic Philology,* 67 (October 1968), 594–611.

E.10 "Style as Meaning in the *Book of the Duchess." Language and Style,* 2 (Spring 1969), 143–71.

E.11 "Cynewulf's *Elene:* Sources and Structure." *Neophilologus,* 54 (January 1970), 65–76.

E.12 "Fulgentius's *Expositio Vergiliana Continentia* and the Plan of *Beowulf:* Another Approach to the Poem's Style and Structure." *Papers on Language and Literature,* 6 (Summer 1970), 227–62.

E.13 "Idea and Emotion in the Towneley *Abraham." Papers on Language and Literature,* 7 (Summer 1971), 227–41.

E.14 "The Way We Write Now." *New York Times Book Review,* 9 July 1972, pp. 2, 32–33. On contemporary fiction.

E.15 "Nicholas Vergette." *Craft Horizons*, 33 (October 1973), 30–33, 65. Profile.

E.16 "Saint Walt: The Greatest Artist the World Has Ever Known, Except for Possibly Apollonius of Rhodes." *New York*, 6 (12 November 1973), 64–71. On Walt Disney.

E.17 "We Teach and Study and Raise All the Hell We Can." Illus. Herbert L. Fink. *Change*, 5 (June 1975), 42–47. Profile of Southern Illinois University at Carbondale.

E.18 "Amber (Get) Waves (Your) of (Plastic) Grain (Uncle Sam)." *New York Times*, 29 October 1975, Sec. M, p. 39. On the Bicentennial Year; condensed and retitled "A Thing Worth Celebrating" in *Reader's Digest*, 108 (April 1976), 136–38.

E.19 "The New Palace of the Arts." *Bennington College Dedicates Its Arts Complex/Bennington Banner*, 21 May 1976, pp. 1–2, 4. Special supplement to the newspaper, edited by John Gardner with Tyler Resch.

E.20 "Moral Fiction." *Hudson Review*, 29 (Winter 1976–77), 497–512. Excerpted from *On Moral Fiction*.

E.21 "Southern Illinois." *Vogue*, 167 (March 1977), 156–57.

E.22 "The Idea of Moral Criticism." *Western Humanities Review*, 31 (Spring 1977), 97–109. Excerpted from *On Moral Fiction*.

E.23 "Death by Art; or, 'Some Men Kill You with a Six-Gun, Some Men with a Pen.' " *Critical Inquiry*, 3 (Summer 1977), 741–71. Excerpted from *On Moral Fiction*.

E.24 "On Dave Smith." *Three Rivers Poetry Journal*, No. 10 (1977), pp. 6–10.

E.25 "John Gardner's Statement Designating the Fiction Award Recipients." *Kansas Quarterly*, 10 (Winter 1978), 6–8. Gardner explains his standards and prejudices in judging short stories.

E.26 "Moral Fiction." *Saturday Review*, 5 (April 1978), 29–30, 32–33. A brief excerpt from *On Moral Fiction*, adapted from chap. 5 and elsewhere.

F. Reviews in Magazines and Newspapers

First publication in magazines and newspapers of reviews by Gardner, arranged chronologically. Illustrated works are noted.

F.1 *Art and Tradition in Sir Gawain and the Green Knight,* by Larry D. Benson. *Journal of English and Germanic Philology,* 65 (October 1966), 706–8. Reprinted in *Critical Studies of Sir Gawain and the Green Knight;* see B.1.

F.2 "An Invective against Mere Fiction." *Southern Review,* NS 3 (Spring 1967), 444–67. Discusses *The Firebugs,* by Peter Faecke; *Dink's Blues,* by Marilyn Hoff; *Home Is Where You Start From,* by Gene Horowitz; *A Night at Sea,* by Margaret Lane; *Let Noon Be Fair,* by Willard Motley; *Bazzaris,* by Don Tracy; *The Double Image,* by Helen MacInnes; *Lionheart,* by Alexander Fullerton; *A Mother in History,* by Jean Stafford; *A Vision of Battlements,* by Anthony Burgess; *Three Novels,* by Willem Elsschot; *Tenants of the House,* by Heather Ross Miller; *The Sailor Who Fell from Grace with the Sea,* by Yukio Mishima; *The House on the Canal,* by Frans Coenen; *Alienation,* by J. Van Oudshoorn; *Mrs. Stevens Hears the Mermaids Singing,* by May Sarton; *Of the Farm,* by John Updike; *After Julius,* by Elizabeth Jane Howard; *The Comedians,* by Graham Greene; *The Encounter,* by Crawford Power; *Miss MacIntosh, My Darling,* by Marguerite Young; *Omensetter's Luck,* by William Gass.

F.3 *The Three Temptations: Medieval Man in Search of the World,* by Donald R. Howard. *Journal of English and Germanic Philology,* 66 (April 1967), 249–54.

F.4 "More Smog from the Dark Satanic Mills." *Southern Review,* NS 5 (Winter 1969), 224–44. Discusses *Indian Summer,* by John Knowles; *The Jubjub Bird,* by William Hardy; *Hog Butcher,* by Ronald L. Fair; *Meanwhile Back at the Henhouse,* by Thomas Bledsoe; *The Late Bourgeois World,* by Nadine Gordimer; *The Decline of the West,* by David Caute; *Alley Jaggers,* by Paul West; *A State of Siege,* by Janet Frame; *The Holy Land,* by Pär Lagerkvist; *Tremor of Intent: An Eschatological Spy Novel,* by Anthony Burgess; *The Gates of the Forest,* by Elie Wiesel.

F.5   "Witchcraft in Bullet Park." Rev. of *Bullet Park*, by John
      Cheever. *New York Times Book Review*, 24 October 1971, pp. 2,
      24.
F.6   "For Young Readers." Rev. of *About Wise Men and Simpletons:
      Twelve Tales From Grimm*, trans. Elizabeth Shub; illus. Nonny
      Hogrogian. *New York Times Book Review*, 31 October 1971, p. 8.
F.7   *Aspects of Alice: Lewis Carroll's Dreamchild as Seen Through the
      Critics' Looking-Glasses, 1865–1971*, ed. Robert Phillips; illus.;
      and *Alice in Wonderland; Authoritative Text of Alice's Adventures
      in Wonderland, Through the Looking-Glass, and the Hunting of the
      Snark (With Backgrounds and Essays in Criticism)*, ed. Donald J.
      Gray; illus. *New York Times Book Review* (30 January 1972), 3–22.
F.8   "Why Do Virginal Old Ladies Keep Cats?" Rev. of *Animals in Art
      and Thought to the End of the Middle Ages*, by Francis Klingender,
      ed. Evelyn Antal and John Harthan; illus. *New York Times Book
      Review* (9 April 1972), pp. 27–28.
F.9   *The Breast*, by Philip Roth. *New York Times Book Review*, 17
      September 1972, 3, 10.
F.10 "Change Was the Church's Dirty Little Secret." Rev. of *Bare
      Ruined Choirs: Doubt, Prophecy, and Radical Religion*, by Garry
      Wills. *New York Times Book Review*, 24 October 1972, pp. 1, 10.
F.11 *Snow-White and the Seven Dwarfs A Tale From the Brothers
      Grimm*, trans. Randall Jarrell; illus. Nancy Ekholm Burkert. *New
      York Times Book Review*, 5 November 1972, pp. 1, 18, 20.
F.12 "They Clapped When He Entered the Classroom." Rev. of
      Wishes, Lies, and Dreams: Teaching Children to Write Poetry, by
      Kenneth Koch; and *Rose, Where Did You Get That Red? Teaching
      Great Poetry to Children*, by Kenneth Koch. *New York Times Book
      Review*, 23 December 1973, pp. 1, 14.
F.13 "The Adventurer." Rev. of *The Fate of Adventure in the Western
      World*, by Paul Zweig. *New York Times Book Review*, 22 De-
      cember 1974, p. 7.
F.14 "The Finest King." Rev. of *The Golden Dragon: Alfred the Great
      and His Times*, by Alfred J. Mapp, Jr. *Harper's Magazine*, 250
      (April 1975), 104–5.
F.15 *Beyond the Bedroom Wall: A Family Album*, by Larry Woiwode.
      New York Times Book Review, 28 September 1975, pp. 1, 2.
F.16 "No Creature So Creative Can be All Bad." Rev. of *The Mythic
      Image*, by Joseph Campbell. *New York Times Book Review*, 28
      December 1975, pp. 15–16.
F.17 "Big Deals." Rev. of *J. R.*, by William Gaddis. *New York Review
      of Books*, 10 June 1976, pp. 35–38, 40.

F.18 *The Doctor's Wife,* by Brian Moore. *Washington Post,* 17 October 1976, Sec. IV, p. 3.

F.19 "The Essential King Arthur, According to John Steinbeck." Rev. of *The Acts of King Arthur and His Noble Knights From the Winchester Mss. of Thomas Malory and Other Sources,* by John Steinbeck, ed. Chase Horton. *New York Times Book Review,* 24 October 1976, pp. 31–32, 34, 36.

F.20 "Leprechaun on the Loose." Rev. of *Mr. Moon's Last Case,* by Brian Patten; illus. Mary Moore. *Washington Post,* 7 November 1976, Sec. G, pp. 5–6.

F.21 "Sinking into Nature." Rev. of *Whole Hog* and *Collected Poems 1956–1976,* by David Wagoner. *New York Times Book Review,* 2 January 1977, pp. 7, 10.

F.22 "The Quest for the Philosophical Novel." Rev. of *Lancelot,* by Walker Percy. *New York Times Book Review,* 20 February 1977, pp. 1, 16, 20.

F.23 "Victorian at Sea." Rev. of *A Fringe of Leaves,* by Patrick White. *Washington Post,* 27 February 1977, Sec. E, p. 9.

F.24 "The Pilgrims' Hair Turned White." Rev. of *The Castle of Crossed Destinies,* by Italo Calvino, trans. William Weaver; illus. *New York Times Book Review,* 10 April 1977, pp. 15, 29.

F.25 *Tsuga's Children,* by Thomas Williams. *New York Times Book Review,* 15 May 1977, pp. 13, 44; see G.6.

F.26 "In Defense of the Real." Rev. of *Daniel Martin,* by John Fowles. *Saturday Review,* 5 (1 October 1977), 22–24.

F.27 "The World of Tolkien." Rev. of *The Silmarillion,* by J. R. R. Tolkien, ed. Christopher Tolkien. *New York Times Book Review,* 23 October 1977, pp. 1, 39–40.

F.28 "John Gardner on Fiction." *New Republic,* 177 (3 December 1977), 33–34. Discusses *David Martin,* by John Fowles; *Going after Cacciato,* by Tim O'Brien; *Song of Solomon,* by Toni Morrison; *Possession,* by Nicholas Delbanco; *Refiner's Fire,* by Mark Helprin.

F.29 "A Cheever Milestone: 61 Elegantly Crafted Stories." Rev. of *The Stories of John Cheever,* by John Cheever. *Book World/ Chicago Tribune,* 22 October 1978, Sec. 7, p. 1.

F.30 "Malamud: A Comedy of Ardors." Rev. of *Dubin's Lives,* by Bernard Malamud. *Book World/Washington Post,* 25 February 1979, Sec. M, pp. 1, 3.

F.31 "A Novel of Evil." Rev. of *Sophie's Choice,* by William Styron. *New York Times Book Review,* 27 May 1979, pp. 1, 16–17; see G.7.

G. Letters in Magazines and Newspapers

G.1   *Chico State Wildcat*, 12 October 1961, p. 4. Letter to the editor, saying that he ended his editorship and publication of *Selection* (a student literary journal) because of administrative censorship.

G.2   "No One Is Being Cheated." *Southern Illinoisan* [Carbondale], 15 September 1975, p. 5. Letter to the editor, supporting research on marijuana and sex.

G.3   "Commercialism Is Not Exactly a Sin." *Bennington Banner*, 15 July 1976, p. 4. Letter to the editor, supporting the policy of the Bennington Summers Jazz Lab.

G.4   *Parabola*, 1 (Winter 1976), 4. Letter to the editor, commenting on the significance of myth.

G.5   *New American Review*, No. 9 (April 1977), pp. 232–35. Letter to the editor, commenting on the theory of character put forth by William H. Gass in No. 7 of the same magazine.

G.6   *New York Times Book Review*, 11 September 1977, p. 56. Gardner responds to a reader's letter criticizing his review of *Tsuga's Children* (see F.25), saying again that he is offended by the writer's sentimentality in this and earlier works.

G.7   *New York Times Book Review*, 22 July 1979, p. 23. Gardner responds to letters criticizing his review of *Sophie's Choice* (see F.31), apologizing for giving away the ending and admitting that he was unfair in his comments on anti-Semitism in Poland.

G.8   *New York Times Magazine*, 12 August 1979, p. 62. Gardner complains that Stephen Singular's published interview (see H.105) tried to portray him as "an interesting *enfante terrible*" by emphasizing Gardner's negative comments about his literary contemporaries, and ignoring the positive. Singular replies that his account of the interview was accurate and objective.

H. Interviews and Speeches

Interviews and speeches in various media, arranged chronologically and annotated as cumulative parts of one interview. Unless the inevitable repetitions are crucial to the context, they are simply noted. Any seemingly contradictory statements are included. Interviews noted as "indispensable" (see H.23, H.87, H.88, H.95, H.96, and H.105) cannot be adequately summarized.

H.1   Harris, Bruce. "Faculty Resignations Rise." *Chico State Wildcat*, 5 April 1962, pp. 1, 9. Briefly quotes Gardner's statement to the Faculty Council.

H.2   "Five Seek Posts on CCHS Board." *Southern Illinoisan* [Carbondale], 7 April 1968, p. 2. Briefly quotes Gardner's statement of purpose in running for the Board of Carbondale Community High School.

H.3   Ryzak, Joan. "U-D's Rebel with Pen—Compleat Wrangler." *Sunday News* [Detroit], 20 December 1970, Sec. B, p. 16. Gardner points to family influences on his writing and comments on *MSS*, his short-lived literary magazine. He says that his stories are unpredictable. They mix ancient forms with modern sensibility and are aimed at the same audience that James Joyce wrote for.

H.4. Diehl, Digby. "Medievalist in Illinois Ozarks." *Los Angeles Times Calendar*, 5 September 1971, p. 43. An interview inspired by the publication of *Grendel* and illustrated with a picture of "John Gardner," the British mystery writer.

Gardner says that contemporary society resembles that of Chaucer and Malory: It stares into an abyss. Chaucer saw the grotesque collapse of his world as black and funny. Malory's *Morte d'Arthur* is a twentieth-century book in its vision. *Grendel* was written in this same pessimistic spirit. It rejects the concept of heroism portrayed in *Beowulf*. Gardner's Grendel is a "Sartre anarchist who kills himself over a momentary failure of ideals." Ultimately, Gardner has nothing to say except that "words are beautiful." He is only concerned with style, with rhythm and rhyme. In this he is like William Gass, Stanley Elkin, Donald Barthelme, John

Barth, Ralph Ellison, and Samuel Beckett. "There are no disturbing philosophies left anymore. We've hit the bottom and we're just bouncing."

H.5   Lair, Bill. "Visiting Authors Say Novels Are Merely Rearranged Facts." *Argus* [Rock Island], 27 November 1972, p. 17.

Gardner, interviewed with Fletcher Knebel, comments briefly on television and the reality of fictional characters.

H.6   Natale, Richard. "John Gardner: 'Great Age of the Novel Is Returning.' " *Women's Wear Daily*, 8 December 1972, p. 16. Reprinted nationally, the interview focuses on *The Sunlight Dialogues*.

The Sunlight Dialogues is written in the epic form: twenty-four books, epic themes and tricks, parallel plots. It makes use of the magician and the wilderness as in medieval romances, while parodying the nineteenth-century novel. Since Gardner does not believe in the God-centered world of Tolstoy, he created a novelist-persona who does: Warburton Hodge. The novel is about creation and dissolution, law and order; about a free man (the Sunlight Man) and a caged man (Clumly). In general the modern novel has swung from the realism of Robert Louis Stevenson and Victor Hugo, to the type of self-conscious works that Henry Fielding created. Capote's *In Cold Blood* is good fiction, not reporting; John Barth's *The Sotweed Factor* is a technically perfect book without heart; William Gass's fiction offers a dramatic new voice; Philip Roth's *Portnoy's Complaint* is a good cartoon autobiography in the Fielding tradition.

H.7   Johnson, Chuck. "John Gardner: Author." *Southern Illinoisan* [Carbondale], 21 January 1973, Sec. A, p. 3.

Gardner discusses his career, his forthcoming work, his views on Kant, Whitehead, and Sartre; and his thematic intentions in *The Resurrection* and *Grendel. The Resurrection* dramatizes the anguish of a man who is unable to think, and the terrifying sense of alienation when one can no longer make connections with the universe. Grendel also experiences a profound sense of alienation but is ultimately forced to feel and as a consequence dies knowing he is connected to the world.

H.8   Davis, Tony. "John Gardner Heroes Include Achilles, Aeneas, Beowulf, Hector . . ." *Daily Northwestern*, 31 January 1973, p. 3.

Gardner speaks of his love for the epic; criticizes Barth, Barthelme, and Vonnegut for their cynicism; praises Bellow and Purdy for their optimism.

H.9 Slyke, Judy Van. "The Scholar Who Wrote a Best Seller."
Chicago Daily News, 7–8 April 1973, p. 4.
Gardner says that his handling of the narrative in *The Sunlight Dialogues* lacks ironic distance.

H.10 Wilder, Alec. "Back to the Roots of That Novelist from Batavia."
Rochester [N.Y.] *Democrat & Chronicle/Upstate Magazine*, 15 April 1973, pp. 20–24. A profile of prototypes for *The Sunlight Dialogues:* Gardner's parents, Mr. and Mrs. John C. Gardner; and his aunt, Mildred Britt. Brief quotes.

H.11 Pratt, Kathie. "Gardner May Use Grant for Year in France."
Daily Egyptian [Southern Illinois University at Carbondale], 24 April 1973, p. 15.
Gardner's comments on receiving the Guggenheim Award.

H.12 Brown, Bill. *Focus.* WBTA Radio [Batavia, N.Y.]. Radio tape: approx. 28 minutes. Interview recorded 28 April 1973 for delayed broadcast.
Gardner dates the composition vs. publication of various novels; points to the literary influences of his apprenticeship, and to the experiential sources of *The Sunlight Dialogues.* Ben and Vanessa Hodge are based on his mother and father; Millie Hodge is based on his Aunt Mildred. T. Murray Steele is the actual name of the doctor in Batavia who inspired Gardner's early interest in the classics.

H.13 Pfalzer, Marilyn. *"The Sunlight Dialogues* Will Soon Be Made into a Movie." *Daily News* [Batavia], 30 April 1973, p. 1. Gardner collaborated with director Jules Dassin on a movie script; it was not produced. Brief quotes.

H.14 ———. "Writing 'Celebrates,' Top Author Asserts." *Daily News* [Batavia], 30 April 1973, pp. 1, 4.
Gardner says that all the characters in *The Sunlight Dialogues* are based on actual people, except for Chief Clumly and the Sunlight Man. He advises young writers to fight against the forces of anarchy in the world, and to celebrate the people they love.

H.15 *Writers on Writing.* Rochester, N.Y.: University of Rochester Writers Workshop, 1973, [pp. 1–14]. A pamphlet, with photographs, distributed by the Writers Workshop at the University of Rochester. The pamphlet transcribes a panel discussion televised by WXXI-TV on 9 July 1973. The members of the panel were: L. J. Davis, moderator; John Gardner, Judith Rascoe, and George P. Elliott.
The panelists discuss American writers' fascination with the

grotesque; their inability to create "grownup" characters; their "American" consciousness; their obsession with technique; their response to reviewers; their belief in creative accidents; their response to the sadism of comic films; and their creative response to films in general. Speaking of the grotesque, Gardner says that he consciously works for it. He wants a novel that is like an animated movie Disney was afraid to do. Unlike the stories of Jean Stafford, his stories are not written with the assumption that they are good for the reader. They are meant to hold the reader's interest like a circus show, like Bugs Bunny, or the Phantom of the Opera. Speaking of the creative process, Gardner says that he consciously seeks the creative "accident." Fred Clumly, the police chief of *The Sunlight Dialogues,* entered Gardner's imagination some 400 pages into another novel. Gardner threw away the novel and began again with Clumly, an "accident."

H.16   Mikkanen, Mildred. "Word Addict." *Rochester* [N.Y.] *Times-Union,* 10 July 1973, Sec. C, pp. 1–2.

Gardner discusses familiar biographical details and his teaching in the University of Rochester's Writers Workshop.

H.17   Flickner, Sandy. "Author John Gardner: A Serious Clown." *Rochester* [N.Y.] *Democrat & Chronicle,* 12 July 1973, Sec. C, pp. 1–2. Describes and quotes Gardner's instructions to Writers Workshop at the University of Rochester.

H.18   Cochrane, Diane. "John Napper: The Return of the Illustrated Novel." *American Artist,* 37 (July 1973), 26–31. A profile of the illustrator of *The Sunlight Dialogues,* which quotes Gardner on illustration.

Henry James erred when he assumed that all mature fiction was realistic and solemn, and that illustrations merely illustrate. Doré gave Dante's hell new dimensions just as Tenniel transformed Lewis Carroll's Wonderland. Napper's illustrations of *The Sunlight Dialogues* are in this great tradition. They freeze complex emotions into charged images. They are, like all great illustrations, not "visions" or "visual ideas," but "fictions."

H.19   Janus, Pat. "Interview: Pat Janus and John Gardner." *Valley Magazine,* No. 1 (September 1973), pp. 21–24.

Gardner repeats his comments on the experiential aspects of *The Sunlight Dialogues* (see H.12, H.14, H.15), and notes the development of the same ideas in *The Wreckage of Agathon* and *Grendel*. And he again discusses the question of illustrations—in this case, those for *Jason and Medeia*, which he feels are "campy" in effect. They were supposed to illustrate the myth of Jason ("intellect") and Medeia ("creativity" or "nature") from ancient Sumer to modern time.

H.20 Hansen, Linda. "Fiction and 'So-Called Reality.' " *Rochester* [N.Y.] *Times-Union*, 1 November 1973, Sec. C, p. 1. Gardner gave this brief interview shortly before making a speech with the same title at the University of Rochester's Wilson Day celebration, 1 November 1973.

Gardner tries to fight the contemporary nihilism and despair by presenting an optimistic view of man.

H.21 "Life Follows Fiction—Never Doubt It." *University of Rochester Currents*, 9 November 1973, pp. 1, 3–4. Prints Gardner's speech ("Fiction and So-Called Reality") delivered at the University of Rochester's Wilson Day celebration, 1 November 1973.

The idea of mechanical reality is destructive; it is a myth that leads to separation. Whitehead's *Process and Reality*, Backster's polygraph experiments with plants, primitive bear worship—all support the idea that all human life is connected. The idea of separateness is supported by the violence and sentimentality of current films and TV shows. One should turn to the celebration of life found in the works of poets like Mona Van Duyn and Howard Nemerov; fiction writers like Stanley Elkin, William Gass, Joyce Carol Oates, and Eudora Welty. One should support the myth of connectedness and deny the "very existence of so-called reality, the myth of blind mechanics."

H.22 Boyd, Robert. "A Writer's Offhanded Dazzle." *St. Louis Post-Dispatch*, 28 November 1973, Sec. F, p. 2. A profile of Gardner based on an interview at the author's residence south of Carbondale. Though the biographical details are familiar, the characterization of Gardner's erudition and sensibility is illuminating.

H.23 Ensworth, Pat, and Joe David Bellamy. "John Gardner: An Interview." *Fiction International*, Nos. 2–3 (1974), pp. 33–40. An indispensable interview, which combines conversations held with Gardner by Pat Ensworth at Northwestern University (Spring 1973) and by Joe David Bellamy at the University of Rochester (10–11 July 1973). Reprinted in *The New Fiction*; see B.11.

Contemporary writers are like Henry Fielding rather than

Victor Hugo. They take on a distinct voice. They create dream-realities rather than the realities of older writers like Hemingway or Faulkner or O'Hara. Gardner has been influenced by Herman Melville, William Gass, Walt Disney, Edgar Allan Poe, and Henry James. He sees a growing optimism in the work of Joyce Carol Oates, John Updike, and John Cheever. And he places himself in a group that includes Stanley Elkin, William Gass, and Donald Barthelme, though he does not agree with either their philosophical or esthetic stances. A writer should, Gardner suggests, make wonderful "sand castles," which are true to experience but do not try to explain experience. Sand castles are moral. They make the reader a better person than any sermon does. "I like Barth's funhouse metaphor. I think it's right. Every writer now is lost in the funhouse—and pretty happy with it." (Note also Gardner's detailed analyses of *Grendel* and *The Sunlight Dialogues.*)

H.24   Mattos, Edward. *Writer in Society: John Gardner.* Color Video Tape: 28 minutes. Washington, D.C.: United States Information Agency, 1974. This interview was taped (date unknown) for broadcast in Japan before and during Gardner's USIS tour, which began 8 September 1974 and ended 5 October 1974. The interview begins with a long introduction stressing biographical and bibliographical details. In general the interview places unusual emphasis—for Gardner—on social and political influences. Gardner discusses Watergate, the destructive impact of American technology, the impact of blacks on the business and literary world. He speaks of Mishima, Tolstoy, and Cervantes in relationship to their social and political influences. He praises Donald Barthelme's fiction and notes the tendency of American writers to escape into fable, to "non-reality," to "non-responsibility." Pointing to the "cop and robber" plot of *The Sunlight Dialogues,* he suggests that if a writer is going to treat a real issue, in terms of real political questions, then he probably has to write a realistic novel.

H.25   "John Gardner." *East West Journal,* 4 (February 1974), 34–35. Gardner emphasizes the need for form, pointing to *Jason and Medeia,* East Indian stories, African stories; and the need for a greater feeling of community to combat the American obsession with spiritually isolating individualism.

H.26 Miyamoto, Yokichi. ["The Star of the 1970's in American Literature: An Interview with John Gardner."] *Yomiuri Shimbun*, 17 September 1974, p. 7. In Japanese.

An unpublished translated paraphrase makes a number of comments about contemporary literature and Gardner's position and reputation; and quotes Gardner as saying that he wrote *Grendel* in the early sixties against the "mainstream of realism," and that it was not published "until over ten years later."

H.27 ["Mr. John Gardner: Visiting American Writer Here to Lecture on Contemporary American Literature."] *Mainichi Shimbun*, 21 September 1974, p. 3. In Japanese.

An unpublished translated excerpt quotes Gardner's praise for the Japanese writers Mishima and Nozaka.

H.28 Kitazawa, Masakuni. ["Downfall and Restoration of American Society: A Dialogue with John Gardner."] *Asahi Journal*, 27 September 1974, pp. 80–85. In Japanese.

An unpublished translated excerpt reveals that Gardner talked about the impact of the Korean and Vietnamese wars; about women's liberation, the evils of capitalism, Watergate, and Ford's mistake in giving Nixon a pardon. He names Saul Bellow and Eudora Welty as his favorite American writers; and Joyce Carol Oates as one of the best younger writers.

H.29 "Powerful Firms Will Destroy Us." *Mainichi Daily News*, 2 October 1974, p. 4. Gardner participated in a panel discussion at the American Center in Osaka. Of the numerous interviews and commentaries printed this seems to be the only one published in English.

Traditional realism lost its meaning when the Vietnam war broke out. He tries to "get rid of everyday reality and get to the heart of guilt, violation and anarchism immediately."

H.30 Iwamoto, Iwao. "John Gardner no Sekai: Taidan to Sakuhin wo Toshite [The World of John Gardner . . .]." *Eigo Seinen* [*The Rising Generation*], 120 (January 1975), 454–55.

An unpublished summary translation suggests it is largely a recapitulation of earlier interviews and their questions and answers—except, perhaps, for Gardner's suggestion that there is a causal relationship between his rural upbringing and his optimism.

H.31 Parker, Gail Thain. "An Interview with John Gardner." *Quadrille* [Bennington College], 4 (Spring 1975), 3–6.

Gardner comments on the early years of his marriage, on his teaching, on Bennington students.

H.32 Askins, John. "Conversations with John Gardner on Writers and Writing." *Detroit Free Press/Detroit Magazine,* 23 March 1975, pp. 19–21. Reprinted in *Authors in the News;* see B.19.
Gardner comments on the literary marketplace, Joyce Carol Oates, Chaucer, family activities, and existentialism. Existentialism can be self-pitying. At his best Jean-Paul Sartre is optimistic, brave, and noble. But he is often terribly wrong in the positions he takes. Gardner has a single philosophical position he is working on. He is asking about the nature of human experience in the twentieth century and how it can be fixed. Once he has treated one aspect of the question, he does not repeat it. "There are very precise points where I think we've gone wrong, and I think I could name them in terms of philosophical schools of thought."

H.33 Dardenne, Bob. "The Gardner Dialogues." *Rochester* [N.Y.] *Times-Union,* 25 March 1975, Sec. C, pp. 1–2. Gardner gave this brief interview shortly after he received an award for *The Sunlight Dialogues* from the Friends of the Rochester Public Library, 24 March 1975. See H.34.
Gardner comments on the autobiographical and experiential aspects of *The Sunlight Dialogues,* noting parallels cited in earlier interviews.

H.34 Prichard, Peter. "Gardner—a Writer at 8?" *Rochester* [N.Y.] *Democrat & Chronicle,* 25 March 1975, Sec. C, pp. 1–2.
This article gives a brief biography and then paraphrases and quotes from Gardner's "ad-lib" speech to the Friends of the Rochester Public Library, 24 March 1975. See H.33.

H.35 Meagher, Tom, and Josh Hanft. "John Gardner Presents 'Shadows.' " *Middlebury Campus,* 24 April 1975, p. 4.
Briefly quotes from Gardner's comments about "Shadows," the working title of a novel about southern Illinois.

H.36 Teicholz, Thomas. "Conversation with John Gardner." *Middlebury Campus,* 24 April 1975, p. 4.
Gardner comments on work habits and book reviewers; and offers advice to beginning writers.

H.37 Blades, Nancy. "A New Novelist in Old Bennington." *Bennington Banner,* 26 April 1975, pp. 1–2. A profile of Gardner and family.
Asked if he would consider Bennington as the setting for a

novel, Gardner answered that he was too new to the area, that he was writing a novel set in southern Illinois ("Shadows," apparently).

H.38 Cross, Leslie. "No Rest for John Gardner." *Milwaukee Journal*, 11 May 1975, Sec. V, p. 4.

Gardner says that modern literature is trivial compared to Dante; good writing is celebration; his life of Chaucer corrects numerous misconceptions.

H.39 Johnson, Ken. "Best-Selling Novelist Talks about Work, SIU." *Daily Egyptian* [Southern Illinois University at Carbondale], 25 August 1975, Sec. B, p. 18.

Gardner discusses his feelings about Southern Illinois University, his plans for a USIS tour of Russia in the spring of 1976, and makes familiar comments about the need for Christian ideals.

H.40 White, Jean M. "The Modern Novel Is an Awful Thing." *Washington Post*, 3 December 1975, Sec. C, pp. 1, 6. Reprinted nationally.

Gardner discusses his move from Carbondale to Bennington, his novel in progress, his proposed tour to Russia for the USIS, and says that the modern novel is boring in its insistence on burying the reader in the subconscious of boring people.

H.41 Quackenbush, Rich. "Dialogue with Gardner in a Sunlit Hotel Room." *Ann Arbor News*, 14 December 1975, p. 30.

Gardner makes some general comments about contemporary fiction, film, and television; and says that he has a novel in progress entitled "Lost Souls' Rock," which is a funny book not designed to change the American character.

H.42 Banker, Stephen. "Tapes for Readers: John Gardner." Audio tape: 16 minutes. Tapes for Readers Series, LIT-025, 1976. Taped on 2 December 1975 and released in 1976 by Stephen Banker, 5078 Fulton Street, N.W., Washington, D.C. 20016. Cassette examined was stamped with a copyright date of "1978."

Though both Fielding's *Tom Jones* and Defoe's *Robinson Crusoe* made fun of the middle-class novel, people didn't listen, and it continues to flourish. As a result, *The Iliad*, *Beowulf*, and the works of Dante are almost lost knowledge, even among university professors. The classical genres were intellectual genres; the modern genres were created so a person can divulge himself. The current preference for nonfiction and journalism, even in a precious magazine like the *New Yorker*, reflects the same interest in gossip that accounts for the popularity of the middle-class novel. Good literature is not simply an attempt to understand the modern age, but all ages. Thus the importance of myths carefully articulated so that a reader will grasp their significance in revealing the truths of mankind. Gardner applies the same esthetic principles to children's fiction as he does to adults' fiction. He simply tries to make sure the fiction is available, or accessible, to younger minds. As a consequence his stories often express the self-doubts and anxieties more commonly found in adult fiction.

H.43 "Distinguished Alumni Citees." *Washington University Alumni News*, 28, No. 1 (Spring 1976), 4–5. Quotes from Gardner's reading of the forthcoming *October Light*, upon receiving a distinguished alumni citation, 6 March 1976.

H.44 Brousseau, Elaine. "Talk with an Author Whose Fiction Tries to Celebrate Goodness." *Providence* [R.I.] *Sunday Journal*, 4 January 1976, Sec. H, p. 19.

Gardner discusses his move to Bennington, deplores the intimacy of the contemporary novel, criticizes the contemporary emphasis on lyric poetry, and applauds the reappearance of the long poem, which requires the poet to put on a voice, to have authority.

H.45 Cackley, Phil. "Gardner Recites From Newest Novel." *Observer* [University of Notre Dame-St. Mary's College], 17 February 1976, p. 1. Gardner appeared with Jorge Luis Borges on a panel during the Sophomore Literary Festival.

He prefaced his reading from *October Light*, and its theme of the failure of communication, by observing that some linguists think that each person has his own language; that men speak a different language than women, and that children speak a different language than adults.

H.46 Bonham, Eupha. "John Gardner Wins Over an Audience." *Bennington Banner*, 20 March 1976, p. 8. Quotes Gardner's brief comments on stories from *Dragon, Dragon* and *A Child's Bestiary*, which he read at Bennington College, 15 March 1976.

H.47 Icen, Richard H. "Carbondale Author John Gardner Advises: Remain Insulated." *Southern Illinoisan* [Carbondale], 28 March 1976, p. 27. Gardner describes early career and current residence in Bennington.

H.48 Marcus, Noreen. "Dragon Eyes Crowd at Novelist's Yard Sale." *Southern Illinoisan* [Carbondale], 10 May 1976, p. 3. Quotes a few of Gardner's amusing comments to friends at a yard sale conducted prior to leaving Carbondale and taking up residence in Bennington. The "dragon" is a ceramic sculpture commissioned by Gardner and placed in a tree in front of his home on Boskydell Road.

H.49 Ephron, Nora. "The Bennington Affair." *Esquire,* 86 (September 1976), 53–151. Quotes Gardner briefly on p. 148.

H.50 Britton, Burt, ed. "Seventeen Self-Portraits." *Harper's Magazine,* 253 (October 1976), 66–67. Reprinted in *Self-Portraits: Book People Picture Themselves;* see B.21.

Gardner's self-portrait is a cartoon of a forest with giant trees and flowers; with a miniature of a dragon's head in the foreground; and with a miniature of Gardner's head peering out from behind a tree in the background.

H.51 Modert, Jo. "John Gardner on Chaucer, Medieval Women, Fairy Tales: An Interview with John Gardner." *St. Louis Post-Dispatch,* 26 December 1976, Sec. E, p. 4.

Gardner discusses his interest in medieval studies, his theory of Chaucer as revealed in his newly published biography, his view of James Page's relationship with his sister Sally in *October Light.*

H.52 "Transcript of Awards Ceremony." *The National Book Critics Circle Journal,* 3 (Spring 1977), 2–6. Prints Gardner's acceptance speech upon receiving The National Book Critics Circle Award for *October Light,* 13 January 1977.

Gardner's speech was in the form of a tall tale about a writer who goes on a free trip to the Bahamas.

H.53 Swindell, Larry. "Our Best Novelist: He Thinks So, Too." *Philadelphia Inquirer,* 16 January 1977, Sec. F, pp. 1, 13. Interview given 23 December 1976.

Gardner comments on work habits, domestic problems, the "genius" of William Gass, Isak Dinesen, Andrey Biely, Hermann Broch, and Alain Robbe-Grillet. He speaks of a current interest in writing opera libretti, of a thematic kinship between *Nickel Mountain* and *October Light,* and of a spiritual kinship with Faulkner and Wolfe.

H.54 Williams, Edgar. "Authors See an Angry Light." *Philadelphia Inquirer,* 20 January 1977.

Briefly quotes Gardner's comments on *October Light* and its protagonist, James L. Page, whom he refers to as a sort of contemporary Everyman.

H.55 Quindlen, Anna. "Why He Writes." *New York Post*, 24 January 1977, p. 25.

Gardner makes some familiar comments about *October Light* and compares his vision and sensibility with that of John Updike, William Gass, and Hilma Wolitzer. Continuing in a personal vein, he mentions a suicidal period of his life that took him "past self-pity into some kind of tragic vision." Though he is a good writer, "there isn't much ego involved anymore. I'm too tired. I sort of write out of grief now."

H.56 White, Jean M. "Books and Authors: Three Speak Out." *Washington Post*, 17 February 1977, Sec. D, p. 9. Briefly quotes Gardner, along with James Dickey and Joseph P. Lash.

H.57 Cuomo, Joseph, and Marie Ponsot. "An Interview with John Gardner." *A Shout in the Street*, 1, No. 2 (1977), 45–63. Gardner gave this interview 12 March 1977.

Gardner praises the work of William Gass and Saul Bellow but faults Gass for doing "linguistic sculptures" instead of fiction. He compares his thematic concern with isolation to that of Joyce Carol Oates and denies any direct debt to Flannery O'Connor, though he notes that they both use caricature, a statement that leads him to credit Disney and discuss sentimentality in American fiction and film. Speaking of individual works, Gardner notes the thematic and tonal relationship between *The Wreckage of Agathon* and *Grendel*; the development of Clumly's character and its relationship to the structure of *The Sunlight Dialogues*; the development of the counterpoint between *The Smuggler's of Lost Souls' Rock* and the primary narrative portraying the "real" world of *October Light*; and the metaphorical significance of the relationship between man and woman as dramatized in *Jason and Medeia*.

H.58 Mable, Sheila. "Behind the Author's Life." *Vermont Cynic* [University of Vermont at Burlington], 17 March 1977, p. 23. Interview given 10 March 1977.

Gardner comments on his teaching and writing career and observes that *Nickel Mountain* is probably the "neatest" and "smoothest" of his works but that *The King's Indian* is probably his "masterpiece."

H.59 ———. "Gardner Fans Grow . . ." *Vermont Cynic* [University of

Vermont at Burlington], 17 March 1977, p. 23. Quotes brief excerpts from Gardner's lecture on "Death by Art," given 10 March 1977; printed—with revision—in *On Moral Fiction*.

H.60 Sachs, Sylvia. "Heritage, God, Schools, Comedy—Authors Cover It All." *Pittsburgh Press*, 14 April 1977, Sec. A, p. 23. Quotes Gardner briefly during a reading from *A Child's Bestiary*.

H.61 Jennes, Gail. "John Gardner Buys Solitude to Unleash the 'Monsters' in His Mind—But at What a Price." *People*, 7 (18 April 1977), 60. A profile based on an interview with Gardner and his family, citing familiar details in hyperbolic terms, and focusing on his move from Bennington to Cambridge, New York, seven months earlier, where he is portrayed as living, separated from his family, in a kind of demonic exile.

H.62 Reddin, Debbie. "John Gardner Speaks on the Moral Aspects of Fiction." *Alabamian* [University of Montevallo], 20 April 1977, p. 4. Quotes brief excerpts from two lectures that Gardner gave 12 April 1977; printed—with revisions—in *On Moral Fiction*.

H.63 Barbato, Joseph. "Novelist and Medievalist: John Gardner on Geoffrey Chaucer." *Chronicle of Higher Education*, 25 April 1977, p. 17.

In an interview occasioned by the publication of *The Life and Times of Chaucer* and *The Poetry of Chaucer*, Gardner discusses his attitude toward scholarship. He says that he is more interested in discovery than argument, and that he has now exhausted his interest in medieval literature.

H.64 Oliven, Cathy, "Interview: Gardner." *Loyola Phoenix* [University of Loyola, Chicago], 29 April 1977, pp. 6, 11. A brief interview with a student reporter unfamiliar with his work.

Plato is right when he says that art is beauty, goodness, and truth, all in one. *Finnegans Wake* is the greatest novel of the twentieth century.

H.65 Mooney, Karen. "Imagination Sole Authority, Novelist Tells Group Here." *Emporia* [Kans.] *Gazette*, 30 April 1977, p. 2. Quotes from a lecture and workshop that Gardner gave at Emporia Kansas State University, 29 April 1977.

Gardner read from *On Moral Fiction* and emphasized his opposition toward the literature of sex and violence, cynicism and despair. "Real art creates myths society can live instead of die by."

H.66 Edwards, Don, and Carol Posgrove. "A Conversation with John Gardner." *Atlantic Monthly*, 239 (May 1977), 43–47. Gardner was interviewed while in Lexington, Kentucky, for the premier of *Rumpelstiltskin,* an opera for which he wrote the libretto. Gardner describes himself as a mixture between a bohemian and a conservative New York State Republican. He discusses his opera *Frankenstein* and the structural and thematic significance of *The Smugglers of Lost Souls' Rock* in *October Light.* And he compares his esthetic stance to that of his friends William Gass and Stanley Elkin. Whereas Gass sees fiction as an object, not apposite to real life, and Elkin sees fiction as entertainment, a performance, Gardner sees fiction as a medium through which "to explore the world and to explain it, to understand it."

H.67 Newall, Robert H. "Author of *Grendel* UMO Guest." *Bangor Daily News,* 7–8 May 1977, p. 6. Gardner gave this interview during the week he spent on the campus of the University of Maine at Orono.

Gardner discusses his work as a librettist, the significance of Disney's *Fantasia* and *Snow White,* the need for art to create and affirm rather than be destroyed by rationalistic theory.

H.68 Chargot, Patricia. "Blasting Away at Today's Top Writers." *Detroit Free Press,* 12 June 1977, Sec. C, p. 5. Paraphrases and quotes from both an interview and a talk that Gardner gave (26 May 1977) at a gathering sponsored by the Friends of the Detroit Public Library.

Gardner criticizes Bellow for placing philosophy before fiction, and Barth for placing fiction before philosophy; and he praises Joyce Carol Oates, John Cheever, Hilma Wolitzer, Rosellen Brown, and Charles Johnson for writing "moral fiction."

H.69 Hoover, Barbara. "Gardner: Words Don't Come Effortlessly." *Detroit News,* 19 June 1977, Sec. L, p. 22.

Gardner discusses the reviews of *October Light;* his work habits; his Welsh-English parentage; his preference for Kobo Abe and Italo Calvino over John Updike, Vladimir Nabokov, Norman Mailer, Saul Bellow, and Joseph Heller. He says that he took up medieval studies, attracted by the fantasy element of the period. "It was a sort of Walt Disney world where dragons were more common than bankers or postmen."

H.70 Dixon, Philip H. "John Gardner: Hard Work, Diversity Mark His Writing." *St. Louis Post-Dispatch/Pictures,* 21 August 1977, p. 11. An interview and profile released by UPI.

Gardner discusses his current teaching activities, his publications on Chaucer, his recent book, *In the Suicide Mountains,* his academic training with Jarvis Thurston at Washington University, his affection for Disney movies, medieval literature, nonrealistic fiction.

H.71 Lague, Louise, "John Gardner & Literature: Just a Loyal Serf in the Kingdom of Words." *Washington Star,* 19 September 1977, Sec. D, pp. 1–2. Describes Gardner in the classroom at George Mason University, his current plans for a NPR series on the arts, and a broadcast of his opera *Rumpelstiltskin.*

Gardner points to John Fowles and Vladimir Nabokov as the best writers of the moment, and notes an upsurge of interest in Chaucer because of his intellect and his largely social and unromantic attitude toward an age much like our own.

H.72 Martin, Rutrell. "Writing of the 70's Is Here but We're Not Seeing It." *College Voice* [Connecticut College], 7 October 1977, p. 5.

Though most artists, whatever their media, are apolitical, their art changes life. Though good writing has texture, great writing also has structure. John Updike's recent work is disappointing. The best writing is either underground or barely recognized like the novels of Tim O'Brien and Charles Johnson.

H.73 Kreitler, Ellen. "Gardner: Grendel Arrives at GMU." *Broadside* [George Mason University], 31 October 1977, p. 4.

Gardner says that he took a position at George Mason University so that he might be in the Washington, D.C. area and work on a series of shows for National Public Radio.

H.74 Allen, Henry. "John Gardner: 'I'm One of the Really Great Writers.' " *Washington Post Magazine,* 6 November 1977, pp. 22–23, 28, 33, 37. Reprinted nationally.

In the light of *On Moral Fiction* Gardner briefly compares the relative merits of Nabokov, Mailer, Bellow, Pynchon, Updike, Salinger, Barthelme, and Barth; praises such nineteenth-century masters as Dostoevsky, Tolstoy, and James; and such classical authors as Dante, Homer, Shakespeare, Chaucer. Asked why his recently published story "Redemption" shuns the "bravura technique of his earlier writing," Gardner is quoted as saying that he has "spent a lot of time evading the dark center of things by, usually, technical tricks."

H.75 Abernathy, Russell. "Religion and Art: 'About the Same Business.' " *Macon News*, 18 November 1977, Sec. B, p. 1. Gardner gave this interview in Macon, Georgia, 16 November 1977, the day after he lectured at Macon Junior College.

Gardner echoes previous statements on art and morality.

H.76 Trotter, Herman. "Novelist John Gardner: Life is Tragic and Joyful." *Buffalo News*, 25 December 1977, Sec. G, p. 2.

Gardner tries to answer questions prompted by statements attributed to him in his interview with Henry Allen of the *Washington Post* (see H.74). Asked, for example, if, as quoted, he has evaded "the dark center of things," Gardner replies that the center is not dark, that there is "life and death at the center," and that he emphasizes the "resurrection of people who have lost touch with their feelings and the realities of life."

H.77 Sklar, Dusty. "Money—Or Your Life?" *Bookviews*, 1 (March 1978), 22, 24.

A number of writers were asked if the mass market lures "serious writers" away from serious work. Gardner says that his work has never been changed to make it more commercial, that his editor at Knopf, Bob Gottlieb, understands his esthetic principles and seldom raises questions that Gardner would not raise himself a year or so later. On the other hand, Gardner adds that he hates "stuff that smacks of academicism. I would never be consciously difficult. I hate Ezra Pound. I'm bored to tears by *Finnegans Wake*. I see nothing but smartaleckiness and arrogance in those things."

H.78 Dell, Twyla. "Dickey, Gardner; 'Impromptu Trialogue,' " *Broadside* [George Mason University], 27 March 1978, pp. 15–16. Describes Gardner's impromptu visit to James Dickey's creative writing class at George Mason University.

The dialogue—or "trialogue"—consists largely of banter between the two friends. Gardner lists the three mistakes most common to writing: "sentimental, frigid, and mannered." He defines "sentimental" writing as that which asks for an effect without giving the cause; "frigid" writing as that which occurs when the writer does not care what is happening to his characters; and "mannered" writing as that which calls attention away from the subject, pointing along with Dickey to Faulkner's "The Bear" as a good story partially flawed by mannered writing.

H.79 "John Gardner." *The Originals: The Writer in America.* Prod. and Dir. Richard O. Moore. PBS, 3 April 1978. Color film: 29 minutes. Produced in 1975 and released in 1978 by Perspective Films, 369 West Erie Street, Chicago, Ill. 60610. Filmed at Gardner's farm near Carbondale and Carroll Riley's home in Carbondale, this valuable profile shows Gardner walking about his farm, talking with friends, and reading from *Grendel, Jason and Medeia*, and *The King's Indian.* See reviews of film in *Booklist*, 75 (1 March 1979), 1098; and *Film News*, 36 (March–April 1979), 21.

H.80 Greenberger, R. E. "A Night with John Gardner: A Private Eye and a Heroine Called Elaine." *Pipe Dream* [State University of New York at Binghamton], 7 April 1978, p. 17. Quotes comments made by Gardner during his reading of novel in progress with the working title "Shadows."

Gardner says that "Shadows," like all his novels, is a "parody." Ross MacDonald's Lew Archer has a scotch every third paragraph but is not a drunk. Gardner's protagonist is a drunk.

H.81 Fuller, Edmund. "A Novelist Calls for Morality in Our Art." *Wall Street Journal*, 21 April 1978, p. 17. Inspired by the publication of *On Moral Fiction*, this interview was conducted at Gardner's residence in Baltimore.

Gardner's only quarrel with religion is that it finds a code that works for a particular group at a particular time. Good art, "moral art," searches for values that are valid for all peoples at all times.

H.82 Howze, John. "Gardner's Paper Gives Insight into Fictional Process." *East Tennessean* [East Tennessee State University], 21 April 1978, p. 6. A review, with brief quotes, of Gardner's reading from his book in progress on the art of writing fiction.

The truth that great fiction seeks is "wordless knowledge."

H.83 Moriarty, Elizabeth. "John Gardner: Good Fiction 'Sets off a Dream . . .'" *Johnson City* [Tenn.] *Press-Chronicle*, 22 April 1978, p. 3. Paraphrases and quotes Gardner's comments to a class at East Tennessee University.

He had once planned to write a book called "The Epic Conversation," an analysis of *The Iliad, The Odyssey, The Aeneid, The Divine Comedy*, and other classics. But instead he entered the epic conversation himself with *Jason and Medeia*. Good fiction, with the possible exception of Homer's, places

character at the center, and as an actor, not a victim. Good
fiction can only happen when the writer, whether moral or
immoral, puts his whole soul into his characters. The reader
should not be reminded of the author; he should be given a
dream that is vivid and continuous.

H.84 Tyler, Ralph. "John Gardner: The Novelist Critic Finds Most of
Today's Fiction Puny." *Bookviews*, 1 (May 1978), 6–9. Occasioned by the publication of *On Moral Fiction*, this interview
was conducted at Gardner's residence in Baltimore.

A conscientious writer may start out with one notion and
arrive at a different conclusion. *October Light* began by
celebrating the "sturdy Vermont values of craftmanship and
honesty." Then an awareness of the negative aspects of this
tradition developed, like a hostility toward people who are
different. The novel traditionally deals with the influence of
the past on a character. Though Sartre's ideas have been a
great influence, he is wrong in his denial of the importance of
history. If one accepts the position that anything can be
changed, that you're free of the past, then fictional character
becomes unimportant.

H.85 Spilka, Mark, ed. "Character as Lost Cause." *Novel: A Forum on
Fiction*, 11 (Spring 1978), 197–217. Gardner is quoted on pp.
212–13.

Gardner was a member of the audience at a panel discussion
on character in fiction held at Brown University in April 1977.
He commented on three different approaches to characterization typified by William Gass, John Hawkes, and Saul Bellow.

H.86 "John Gardner." In *Conversations with Writers*, Vol. I. Detroit:
Gale Research, 1978, pp. 82–103. Interviewed in June 1977 by
C. E. Frazer Clark, Jr.

A wide-ranging interview perhaps most important for its
autobiographical details. Gardner discusses his early literary
influences (Shakespeare, Scott, Dickens); his political and
social conservatism; his scholarly and critical concerns; his
interests in other media (Disney, opera, ballet); his teaching
experiences (at Southern Illinois University, Northwestern
University; Bennington, Williams, and Skidmore colleges).
He responds to questions about the forthcoming publication
of *On Moral Fiction*—at this time called "Thor's Hammer: A
Literary Manifesto." And he comments briefly on Mailer,
Pynchon, Updike, Italo Calvino, Tom Williams, John Jakes,

Charles Johnson, and Mark Helprin. Asked how he would like to be remembered, Gardner answers: "As the greatest librettist of the twentieth century."

H.87 Harvey, Marshall L. "Where Philosophy and Fiction Meet: An Interview with John Gardner." *Chicago Review*, 29 (Spring 1978), 73–87. An indispensable interview.

The interviewer phrases questions that reveal Gardner's philosophical interests and concerns (Plato, Augustine, Aquinas, Nietzsche; but particularly Whitehead and Sartre); his literary interests and esthetic (Homer, Chaucer, Blake, Dickens, Dostoevsky, Melville, Tolstoy, Faulkner, Fowles; but particularly Keats and Coleridge); and his creative intentions (*The Wreckage of Agathon, Grendel, Nickel Mountain;* but particularly *The Resurrection, The King's Indian,* and *In the Suicide Mountains).*

H.88 Natov, Roni, and Geraldine DeLuca. "An Interview with John Gardner." *The Lion and the Unicorn: A Critical Journal of Children's Literature* (Brooklyn, N.Y.), 2, No. 1 (1978), 114–36.

An indispensable interview that helps to illuminate Gardner's ambivalent responses to Sartre's existentialism as well as Gardner's experiential, thematic, and formal approaches to such children's fictions as *Dragon, Dragon, Gudgekin the Thistle Girl, The King of the Hummingbirds,* and *In the Suicide Mountains;* and such major novels as *Grendel, The Sunlight Dialogues, Nickel Mountain,* and *October Light.*

H.89 Nugent, Tom. "Two Literary Lions Tangle." *Baltimore Sun,* 2 May 1978, Sec. B, pp. 1, 6. Describes a meeting between Gardner and John Barth. See Barth's letter of reply: "Li'l Ole Pussycat." *Baltimore Sun,* 6 May 1978, Sec. A, p. 14.

An entertaining account of a low-key but spirited literary debate between Gardner and John Barth, when Gardner attended Barth's seminar in creative writing. Briefly summarizing the thesis of *On Moral Fiction,* and noting that Barth's work received some of Gardner's harshest criticism, the reporter ironically describes and quotes the two authors' disagreement over literary values and terms, particularly those which reflect negatively on Barth's fiction and esthetic.

H.90 Cavett, Dick. *Dick Cavett Show.* PBS, 16 May 1978. TV tape: approx. 28 minutes. Interview recorded a few weeks earlier.

In an interview occasioned by the recently published *On Moral Fiction* Gardner is asked to elaborate on his thesis that life follows art, that good fiction affirms and celebrates. In doing so, he defends his published comments on Barthelme, Bellow, Mailer, and Vonnegut; and praises Fowles's *Daniel Martin* and Tolstoy's *Anna Karenina*.

H.91 Laskin, Daniel. "Challenging the Literary Naysayers." *Horizon*, 21 (July 1978), 32–36. Includes recent photograph.

A profile based on an interview, this article offers a valuable introduction to readers unfamiliar with Gardner and his work. Inspired by the publication of *On Moral Fiction*, the article surveys Gardner's career and offers insights into his themes, influences, and esthetic. Probably most significant is Gardner's statement about *The Sunlight Dialogues:* "What I did in *Sunlight Dialogues* was find a system, a governing metaphysical system that I believe. What I've been doing ever since is pursuing small aspects of the governing system."

H.92 Rutherford, Glenn. "John Gardner: A Writer Who Knows His Craft." *Louisville Courier-Journal*, 15 September 1978, Sec. E, p. 6.

Gardner praises *Anna Karenina*, *Moby-Dick*, "Bartleby the Scrivener," and the *Iliad*; and describes his hallucinatory experience in writing *Nickel Mountain*.

H.93 Allen, Bill. "His 'Vivid Dream' May Well Put You To Sleep." *Dallas Times Herald*, 13 November 1978, pp. 1, 8. Quotes and summarizes Gardner's reading of two stories at Southern Methodist University on 10 November 1978.

Gardner read "The Library Horror" (see C.26) and "Amarand" (see C.27). "The Library Horror" was written, the reporter suggests, to "improve author William Gass's literary theories." "Amarand," a more realistic story, concerns the profound empathy of a symphony conductor for a terminally ill girl who " 'could have been his daughter.' " Both stories were, the reporter feels, "vague, disjunct, and evocative perchance of sleep but not of dreams."

H.94 LeClair, Thomas. "William Gass and John Gardner: A Debate on Fiction." *New Republic*, 180 (10 March 1979), 25, 28–33. This discussion between Gass and Gardner took place on 24 October 1978. In essence it formalizes their debate of some twenty years about the nature of character and the purpose of fiction.

Gardner says that he wants to create lifelike characters in a sustained dream that communicates the feeling as well as the idea of the affirmative values that he discovers in exploring his narrative impulse. Gass, on the other hand, says that he sees a character in a book as a "linguistic location," which parts of the text will modify; that he finds it "convenient not to believe things"; and that he has "very little to communicate."

H.95 Christian, Ed. "Interview with John Gardner." *New York Arts Journal*, No. 14 (1979), pp. 17–19. An indispensable interview. Gardner makes some familiar comments about the corrupting power of cynicism, the invalidity of situational ethics, the literary strengths of his friend William Gass. But he also offers some illuminating insights into the significance of medieval literature in his work, of the grotesque, of love, and of ideas, noting the inspiration he received from reading John M. Cuddihy's book *The Ordeal of Civility*. Even more significant are Gardner's comments on the thematic purpose of *The Resurrection*; on what he feels was a failure to bridge the gap between realism and mythic cartoon in *The Wreckage of Agathon*; on his moment of inspiration for *Grendel*; and on his shift in attitude toward the character of James Page in *October Light*.

H.96 Ferguson, Paul F., John R. Maier, Frank McConnell, and Sara Matthiessen. "John Gardner: The Art of Fiction LXXIII." *Paris Review*, 21 (Spring 1979), 36–74. An indispensable interview, incorporating three interviews conducted with Gardner over a period of about five years. The earliest interview was conducted by Frank McConnell while Gardner was a visiting professor for the winter quarter of 1973 at Northwestern University (cf. H.23). The second interview was taken from a video-taped interview conducted by Paul Ferguson and John Maier at the State University of New York College at Brockport, 6 October 1977. The third interview was conducted by Sara Matthiessen in the spring of 1978 at the Bread Loaf Writers' Colony. The synthesis was read and annotated by Gardner. The publication includes a manuscript page from *Vlemk: The Box-Painter*.

Gardner says that he is bored by psychologically and sociologically oriented plots; that he is inspired by philosophers like R. G. Collingwood, Brand Blanshard, C.D. Broad, and Richard Swinburne; and by philosophical novelists like Tolstoy, Sartre, Beckett, and William Gass, whose work he has sometimes parodied, as in *The Resurrection* (Tolstoy); *Grendel* and *The Wreckage of Agathon* (Sartre); and *Jason and Medeia* (Gass). He points, as well, to the tension he hoped to create in

The Sunlight Dialogues by associating Dante with Chief Fred Clumly and Malory with the persona telling the story; and he points to the symbolic and characterizing aspects of setting in *The Resurrection, The Sunlight Dialogues, Nickel Mountain, The King's Indian,* and *October Light.* Almost all of the first-rate writers of the moment are, he maintains, associated with universities, with the notable exceptions of William Gaddis and John Updike, whose novel *Couples* is given a symbolic analysis. Gardner's story "Redemption" was atypical in its use of autobiographical details—a successful attempt to "ground" the nightmare of his brother Gilbert's death. Additional comments in the interview shed further light on Gardner's opinion of Barth, Dostoevsky, Faulkner, Fitzgerald, Fowles, and Joyce.

H.97 Harkness, James. "Interview: John Gardner." *Forum/The News* [State University of New York], 8 (April 1979), F1–2, F7–9. Gardner discusses the techniques of teaching creative writing, the opportunities for a career, his own apprenticeship. And he further illuminates his notion of moral fiction by citing Céline, who, despite his gifts for grotesque humor, is a "moral" failure, and thus an "esthetic" failure. By the same token, he argues that Merseault of Camus's *The Stranger* is a "morally committed man" rather than a "monster," as the interviewer suggests. But it is Gardner's ambivalent response to Camus's colleague that is best illuminated. Noting that the narrator of Gardner's "The Warden" ends by quoting the opening sentence of Sartre's *Being and Nothingness*, the interviewer asks Gardner if it is necessary for the reader to notice the allusion in order to experience the story fully. Gardner answers that the story works by its plot and emotion, and that the allusion merely gives the potential for a "double pleasure." The interviewer suggests that Gardner is reacting in his fiction to ideas held by Sartre in earlier years and works, and that Sartre's later works, such as *What Is Literature?* and *Critique of Dialectical Reason,* actually argue for a sense of the past and a committed literature. Gardner agrees that he has responded far more extensively to Sartre's early writings but that he keeps "picking on Sartre" because he keeps reading him. "He's one of the greatest writers who ever lived; he's a *beautiful* stylist. That's why it's important to make fun of him."

When he presents a position as he does on the brute existent, which is so moving because of the gorgeous image of the Alp, you have to show what that position becomes when you substitute a vulgar or disgusting image. Then the argument doesn't hold any more."

H.98   Summers, Patty, and Steven Riddle, eds. "Symposium on Fiction." *Phoebe* [George Mason University], 8 (April 1979), 81–83. The editors indicate that they took Gardner's comments from a writers' workshop at George Mason University's January Writers' Conference and integrated them with those of three other writing teachers (Katherine Patterson, Liz Rosenberg, and Susan Shreve) to create the effect of a "symposium."

Gardner offers his familiar definition of good fiction as that which creates a "vivid and continuous dream" and suggests that the plot gives the character the opportunity for self-discovery.

H.99   ———, eds. "Conversation with John Gardner." *Phoebe* [George Mason University], 8 (April 1979), 83–85. Gardner gave this interview while attending George Mason University's January Writers' Conference.

Gardner discusses the techniques of teaching creative writing, and the stages that most writers go through in mastering their craft. He notes that his favorite Disney movies are *Pinnochio, Bambi*, and *Snow White*, and observes that Chaucer was like an extremely intelligent Disney. He credits Chaucer with leading him away from reading contemporary novels to history, theology, and languages; and from there to the adoption of the older genres. Thus *Jason and Medeia* is an imitation epic in the way Chaucer's *Troilus and Criseyde* is; and like Chaucer's narrator, Gardner's narrator steps in and out of the story, getting involved and emotional. By the same token, Gardner was teaching Thomas Malory while writing *The Sunlight Dialogues*, and Malory's symbolic way of thinking similarly informs the novel. Though *The Sunlight Dialogues* has a twentieth-century setting and people, the impetus and emotion of it are in the spirit of the fifteenth century. "I'm working with an ancient tradition that sort of happens to have been written in the twentieth century. It gives a special kind of color to my work."

H.100 Harris, Daisy. " 'Odd Couple' of One Mind on Writing."
    Dayton Daily News, 27 April 1979. Gardner and John Jakes
    were paired for a discussion at a Writers' Workshop sponsored
    by the Sinclair Community College in Dayton, Ohio.
        The authors praised each other highly and stressed the need
    to build strong fictional characters.
H.101 Krisher, Trudy. "Jakes and Gardner: 'We're like Ice Cream
    and Beefsteak; Sometimes You Need One, Sometimes the
    Other.' " *Dayton Journal Herald*, 28 April 1979. Reports on the
    meeting of the two authors at the Sinclair Community College
    Writers' Workshop (see H.100). The quote in the title is taken
    from one of Gardner's comments.
H.102 Grills, Robert. "Contemporary Author Emphasizes Mastery."
    UT [University of Tennessee] Daily Beacon, 10 May 1979, pp. 1,
    6.
        Gardner compares his interest in playing with genre to that
    of a jazz musician, and the necessary process of revision to
    that of a charcoal artist.
H.103 Renwick, Joyce, and Howard Smith. "An Interview with John
    Gardner." *Lone Star Book Review*, 1 (June 1979), 5, 10. Excerp-
    ted from *John Gardner: An Interview*, forthcoming from New
    London Press (October 1979).
        Gardner discusses the potential of radio drama: the recently
    expanded capacity of sound technology, the ability to create
    emotion through the energy of sound rather than solely
    through dialogue. Whereas television can produce every-
    day realism, radio can produce the fabulous world of
    dragons and strange peoples. In writing radio plays such as
    The Temptation Game, which he summarizes, Gardner tries
    to avoid narration and throw the listener right into the
    scene, letting the listener figure out who he is and who he
    likes.
H.104 ————. "Last of the Radio Heroes." *Horizon*, 22 (July
    1979), 67–71. Essentially the same interview as above (H.103),
    though the excerpt begins slightly earlier and makes a number
    of cuts in Gardner's responses.
H.105 Singular, Stephen. "The Sound and Fury over Fiction." *New
    York Times Magazine*, 8 July 1979, pp. 13–15, 34, 36–39. An
    indispensable interview occasioned by the publication of *On
    Moral Fiction* and quoting the reactions of some of the writers
    that Gardner discussed.

Gardner comments on Updike, Malamud, Barthelme, Mailer, and Heller (see G.8). Juxtaposed are comments about Gardner and his thesis by Barth, Hugh Kenner, Updike, Bellow, Malamud, Heller, and William Gass, whose previously published debate with Gardner (see H.94) is partially reprinted. In addition the interviewer notes that Gardner's thesis is anticipated by the earlier statements of critics John Aldridge and Leslie Fiedler; and he discusses three of Gardner's novels—*Grendel, The Sunlight Dialogues,* and *October Light*—finding that Gardner does not follow his own dictum. Perhaps more informative are some of the parallels drawn between Gardner and Tolstoy, and some of the candid and revealing remarks that Gardner makes about his psychological responses to life, about the "weaknesses" of his style in *Nickel Mountain* and, throughout his novels, his failure to portray "real sexual love," a failure he hopes to rectify in his novel-in-progress, "Shadows."

H.106 Renwick, Joyce, and Howard Smith. "An Interview with John Gardner." *Gargoyle,* No. 11 (1979), pp. 5–7. This interview took place on 25 August 1978, at the Bread Loaf Writers' Conference.

On Moral Fiction is aimed at readers who have turned away from fiction because fiction "has gotten boring and stupid and depressing, and shoddy, in many ways." Books by Pynchon and Barth are praised as "true and noble" works of art. But they have very specific faults in them—of execution as well as conception. Academics praise books like Pynchon's *Gravity's Rainbow* because they provide intellectual games for the classroom, whereas, by contrast, the great novels of Trollope and Dickens require little or no explanation. The result of this academic bias is that there is a proliferation of college courses "about books that are easy to teach, because they're arcane, or they're weird, or something else." This is not to say, however, that difficult books like *Finnegans Wake, Ulysses,* and *The Sound and the Fury* are not great, and not worth teaching. Turning to his own work, Gardner says that there is a total theme in his work, "a sort of intuitive artistic metaphysic." Each work represents a part of that metaphysic in a different way. *Grendel,* for example, is essentially about faith and reason dramatized under different headings, such as faith in heroism, faith in love. Finally, at the end of the novel, Grendel—a monster, because he does not believe in anything, has reasoned everything out of existence—makes the leap of faith "because he's sort of pushed over the ledge and driven to it. So that's a book of faith." On the other hand, the stories of *The King's Indian* are "all about art." And *Jason and Medeia* is about "mystical intuity" and the polarities of male and female that exist in the original myth. Asked to name the works that he feels were most successful in realizing his intention, Gardner points first to *The King's Indian*, and then to *The Sunlight Dialogues, Grendel,* and *Nickel Mountain* (which he rewrote "hundreds of times" over a period of "20 years"). But despite the success of these and other works, he has still not made enough money that he does not "have to teach." The interview ends with Gardner's praise for stories read at the Bread Loaf Conference by Susan Shreve, a young writer, and Stanley Elkin, "an old pro."

H.107 Harvey, Marshall. "John Gardner: Considerations . . ." *The Cresset*, 42 (September 1979), 19–22.

Fiction ought to create heroic characters, figures in some way nobler than most people. The best fiction is written by authors willing to take risks. His dissertation, "The Old Men," is terrible because, though it has good characters, it ends up saying something he doesn't believe. In his published novels he uses cartoon images as a way of seeing, as in *The Sunlight Dialogues,* where the association of a mole with Chief Clumly suggests the way he burrows into a set of rules and avoids what he knows to be the truth. Cartoon analogues also inform *Grendel,* "The Ravages of Spring," "The Warden," and the "Tales of Queen Louisa." In his writing he tries to keep a balance between ideas, rhythms, and descriptive details. Sometimes dream-language gives him the first draft of a story or part of a novel, as in "The Ravages of Spring," *Jason and Medeia,* and parts of *The Wreckage of Agathon* and *Grendel.* His reading is generally ecletic. He likes to read philosophy and pore over Faulkner and Melville, but not Hemingway. He believes that Céline is a brilliant writer but wrongheaded morally. He likes to read popular science by writers like Isaac Asimov, and he synthesizes such readings in novels like his work-in-progress

"Shadows." Also of current interest, though he doesn't accept the theory, is psycho-history, which he has worked into another novel-in-progress "Rude Heads that Stare-squint." He was aware of Faulkner's "The Bear" when he created the bear in *October Light*. But Faulkner's bear was less important than the mythic bears associated with the Greek gods, such as Artemis, whose name means "bear" in Greek. More important is the idea that when a hunter kills a bear he separates himself from spirit-nature, and that in order to regain a oneness with nature, he must go through a ritual with the bear. By the same token, there are legends that portray the bear as an eternal creature, able to return from death, which makes the bear "at least a potential Christ figure." The only god that counts is the god of love, and in *October Light*, James Page's reconciliation with spirit-nature is symbolized by his confrontation with the bear, which talks to him—as if Page had "fallen into a dream"—with the voice of his wife.

"That face! . . . that face! Where have I seen that face?"

I. Miscellaneous: Blurbs, Cartoons, Journals Edited, Libretti, Manuscripts, Playbills, Radio Plays, Transcriptions

Blurbs

I.1 Johnson, Charles. *Faith and the Good Thing.* New York: Viking Press, 1974.

I.2 Newman, Charles. *There Must Be More to Love than Death: Three Novellas.* Chicago: Swallow Press, 1976.

I.3 Wolitzer, Hilma. *In the Flesh.* New York: William Morrow & Company, 1977.

Cartoons

I.4 "That face!" *Seventeen Magazine* (July 1948), p. 82. This was, perhaps, Gardner's first professional publication.

I.5 *MSS,* 2 (1964), cover; copyright page; p. 50. Four small, stylized drawings of birds, with the initials "J.G.," appear on the cover; a larger version of the same bird appears on the copyright page; and four stylized drawings of men, echoing the birds, appear on p. 50. Gardner was editor of this journal; see I.7 and also B.21 and H.50.

Journals Edited

I.6 *Selection,* Nos. 1, 2 (1960–61). By Gardner and Lennis Dunlap.

I.7 *MSS,* I, Nos. 1, 2 (Summer 1961–Winter 1962); 2 (1964). By Gardner and others.

Libretti

I.8 *Rumpelstiltskin.* Music by Joseph Baber. Prod. Phyllis Jenness. Opera Workshop of the University of Kentucky School of Music. Lexington Opera House. Lexington. 21–23 January 1977. This opera was given its professional premiere by The Opera Company of Philadelphia at the Walnut Street Theatre (26–30 December 1978) and annual performances are planned.

Manuscripts

I.9 Morris Library, Southern Illinois University at Carbondale. Currently on deposit are ribbon copies and final drafts of

Grendel, The Sunlight Dialogues, and *Nickel Mountain;* late drafts of *The Wreckage of Agathon* and *The King's Indian;* early drafts of *The Resurrection* and *Jason and Medeia;* various drafts of critical and scholarly books; letters, notes, juvenilia.

Playbills

I.10   A. W. S./Presents/THE CAUCUS RACE/Book and Lyrics by John Gardner/Music and Orchestration by/BILL KENNAUGH/With Additional Songs by/NANCY FORD/1954 MONON REVUE [Produced February 11–13, 1954, at DePauw University.]

I.11   OPERA WORKSHOP/presents/The Premiere of/ RUMPELSTILTSKIN/A Comic Opera/in Two Acts, Opus 42/by JOSEPH BABER/on a Libretto by/JOHN GARDNER/Produced by PHYLLIS JENNESS/THE LEXINGTON OPERA HOUSE/ January 21–23, 1977 [Performed in Lexington, Kentucky.]

Radio Plays

I.12   "The Temptation Game." *Earplay.* Dir. Karl Schmidt. NPR. Taped to be broadcast between 1 January 1978 and 1 July 1980. Forthcoming: "The Water Horse." *Earplay.*

Transcriptions

I.13–16 are from DLC, National Library Service for the Blind and Physically Handicapped (Washington, D.C.). I.17–22 are from Recordings for the Blind, Inc. (New York, N.Y.). Please note that discs and tapes are recorded at varying rpm's and require special equipment supplied by the distributors.

I.13   *Grendel* in Braille, No. BR 01772.
I.14   *The Sunlight Dialogues* on disc, No. RD 6700.
I.15   *Nickel Mountain: A Pastoral Novel* on disc, No. RD 7061.
I.16   *October Light* on tape, No. RC 10669.
I.17   *The Forms of Fiction* on tape, No. TL15(07).
I.18   *Grendel* on tape, No. TW704(01).
I.19   *The Sunlight Dialogues* on tape, No. AE166(08).
I.20   *Nickel Mountain: A Pastoral Novel* on tape, No. AG617(03).
I.21   *Jason and Medeia* on tape, No. AF403(05).
I.22   *The Complete Works of the Gawain-Poet* on tape, No. 65-17291.

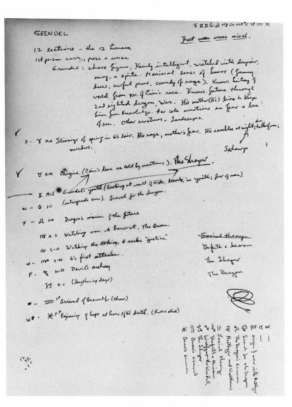

An outline for *Grendel*

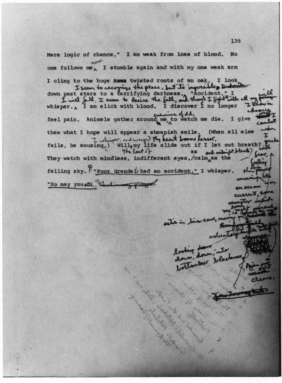

From a late draft of *Grendel*; see novel, pp. 173–74

From a late draft of *The Sunlight Dialogues;* see novel, pp. 94–95

From an early draft of "The Devil"; see *Nickel Mountain,* p. [145]

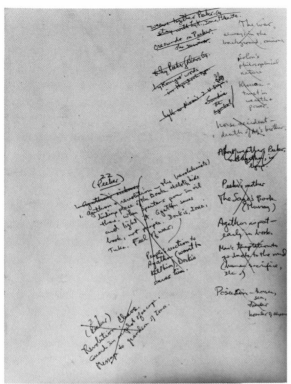

Notes for *The Wreckage of Agathon*

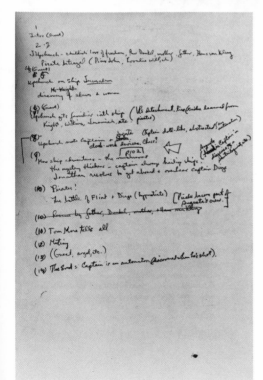

Outline for "The King's Indian" novella

Illustrated by Herbert L. Fink
John Gardner as Jonathan Upchurch
in ''The King's Indian'' novella

1. Kreon, Ipnolidos, + narrator as the storm approaches (p4 ff.)

[p4ff] Kreon bald, grossely fat + reddened, baggy eyed — one eye
squinch shut, other like a diamond. Landscape dark,
in Greek. Ipnolidos extremely bent + shrivelled,
malevolent (see moon-goddess' hemwik, p438).
Narrator in modern dress — black hat + coat, glasses.
If city is shown at all, should be as much
medieval as Greek (probably).

2. Medeia, 2 twin boys, old black slave in garden, Jason
[p24ff] perhaps at window above (with narrator?). M has long
red hair, a beautiful + gentle face but one capable of
transformation to that of a mad + deadly witch.

OR: Medeia + raven [p42ff]

3. Zeus + Hera, perhaps other gods.

4. Medeia, Aygyotika (narr?)

5. Koprophoros and/or Paidoboron? Koupies with Knife?

6. The Argo + Argus? (102f) Whole crew? (1074)
   The Sibyl of Argos (110) The sacrifice (117) Embarkation (123)

7. Jason + Hypsipyle? (149)

8. The squinder men (165ff)

9. Herakles + the tree (176ff) The emmons land (182)
   Polydeukes + king Amykos (184ff)

10. Phineus (196). Ph + the harpies (204ff)

11. Argo + ships from the future (212ff)
    Orpheus in Hell (222f)

12. Shipwrecked sons of Phrixos (242)
    The great serpent (247)

13. The goddesses in the shielded hall? (e 58ff)

14. Jason + the bulls? (300f)

15. Capture of the Fleece? (307f)
    Murder of Apsyrtos (321f)

16. The river god (326f) Circe (330f)

17. Narr in sailors' suit ? (342f). Sirens (350f) Wandering Rocks
    portage in Libya (360); Death of Mopsos (364) (353f)

18. Medeia's witchcraft + (320ff); Murder of Alkestis (389)

19. Jason + Ipnolidos (395f), J + Koupios (347f) J + Tiresias (402f)
    Pyripta + the slave (404f)

20. Koprophoros + or Paidoboron (418ff), J + Pyripta? (439f)
    Narr + double (443)

21. Narr + Zeus? (453f); Narr + Hekate (455f) double? (457)

22. Medeia 460? Argo in to heaven (464), Kreon + Medeia (466f)
    the transmogrification (475f)

23. Medeia into dragon chariot with dead sons, Jason below (495f)

24. Odysseus, mad Ixion, Lynkeus, Jason

IT'S *Please return*

RENDEZVOUS

TIME!!

It was really good. He feels he learned much from its weaknesses too -- mainly a slow second act

A. W. S.

Presents

THE CAUCUS RACE

Book and Lyrics by John Gardner

Music and Orchestration by
BILL KENNAUGH
With Additional Songs by
NANCY FORD

1954 MONON REVUE

Chorus Supervision . . . . Pat Moriarty
Technical Director . . . . Val Loomis
Dramatic Director . . . . Jackie Horner
Co-Ordinate Director . . . . Judy Kent
Publicity . . . Alpha Delta Sigma -- Norm Strasma

UNIVERSITY OF KENTUCKY

SCHOOL OF MUSIC

OPERA WORKSHOP

presents

The Premiere of

RUMPELSTILTSKIN

A Comic Opera
in Two Acts, Opus 42
by JOSEPH BABER
on a Libretto by
JOHN GARDNER

Produced by
PHYLLIS JENNESS

THE LEXINGTON OPERA HOUSE
January 21-23, 1977

J. Articles and Essays
on John Gardner
and His Works

First publication in books and magazines of articles and essays on Gardner and his works, arranged alphabetically. All reprintings and excerpts in *Contemporary Literary Criticism (CLC)* are noted.

J.1   Allen, Bruce. "Settling for Ithaca: The Fictions of John Gardner." *Sewanee Review*, 85 (Summer 1977), 520–31. Review essay of all major works published through 1976, including Gardner's epic, *Jason and Medeia;* see *CLC*, VIII, 236–39.

J.2   Arnold, Marilyn. "*Nickel Mountain:* John Gardner's Testament of Redemption." *Renascence*, 30 (Winter 1978), 59–68.

J.3   Bellamy, Joe David. "The Way We Write Now." *Chicago Review*, 25, No. 1 (1973), 45–49. Article in reply to Gardner's essay "The Way We Write Now," *New York Times Book Review* (see E.14).

J.4   *Contemporary Authors.* Vols. 65–68. Detroit: Gale Research, 1977, p. 241.

J.5   *Contemporary Literary Criticism.* Vol II. Detroit: Gale Research, 1974, pp. 150–53.

J.6   *Contemporary Literary Criticism.* Vol. III. Detroit: Gale Research, 1975, pp. 184–88.

J.7   *Contemporary Literary Criticism.* Vol. V. Detroit: Gale Research, 1976, pp. 131–35.

J.8   *Contemporary Literary Criticism.* Vol. VII. Detroit: Gale Research, 1977, pp. 111–16.

J.9   *Contemporary Literary Criticism.* Vol. VIII. Detroit: Gale Research, 1978, pp. 233–39.

J.10   Cowart, David. "John Champlin Gardner, Jr." In *American Novelists Since World War II.* Vol. II of *Dictionary of Literary Biography.* Ed. Jeffrey Helterman and Richard Layman. Detroit: Gale Research, 1978, pp. 75–85. An essay on Gardner's life and work, with two photographs of Gardner and a facsimile of an early draft of the beginning of *Grendel.*

J.11   Ditsky, John. "The Man in the Quaker Oats Box: Characteristics of Recent Experimental Fiction." *Georgia Review*, 26 (Fall 1972), 297–313. Discusses *Grendel*, pp. 297, 306–8.

J.12   Ellis, Helen B., and Warren U. Ober. "Grendel and Blake: The
        Contraries of Existence." *English Studies in Canada*, 3 (Spring
        1977), 87–102.

J.13   Fitzpatrick, W. P. "Down and Down I Go: A Note on Shelley's
        Prometheus Unbound and Gardner's *Grendel*." *Notes on Con-
        temporary Literature*, 7 (January 1977), 2–5.

J.14   ———. "John Gardner and the Defense of Fiction." *Bulletin of
        the West Virginia Association of College English Teachers*, NS 4
        (Spring 1978 [1977]), 19–28. Discusses *The King's Indian* and
        October Light.

J.15   Groth, Janet. "Fiction vs. Anti-fiction Revisited." *Com-
        monweal*, 106 (11 May 1979), 260–71. Discusses *On Moral
        Fiction*.

J.16   Hendin, Josephine. *Vulnerable People: A View of American
        Fiction Since 1945*. New York: Oxford University Press, 1978,
        pp. 24–25; 133–40; 142, 218, 221. Discusses *Grendel, Jason and
        Medea, Nickel Mountain, October Light*, "The Shape Shifters
        of Shorm," and *The Sunlight Dialogues*.

J.17   Hutman, Norma L. "Even Monsters Have Mothers: A Study
        of *Beowulf* and John Gardner's *Grendel*." *Mosaic*, 9 (Fall 1975),
        19–31.

J.18   Levine, George. "The Name of the Game." *Partisan Review*,
        42 (Spring 1975), 291–97. Review essay of *The King's Indian*,
        drawing on previous novels, excepting *The Wreckage of
        Agathon*.

J.19   McConnell, Frank. "The Corpse of the Dragon: Notes on
        Postromantic Fiction." *Tri-Quarterly*, 33 (Spring 1975), 273–
        303. Discusses *The Resurrection, Grendel, Jason and Medeia*, pp.
        300–303; see *CLC*, VI, 115.

J.20   ———. "Gardner, John (Champlin, Jr.)." In *Contemporary
        Novelists*. Ed. James Vinson. 2nd ed. New York: St. Martin's
        Press, 1976; London: St. James Press, 1976, pp. 491–94. Short
        critical-biographical essay on Gardner's works through *The
        King's Indian*.

J.21   Midwood, Barton. "*The Wreckage of Agathon*." *Esquire*, 74
        (January 1971). Review essay with biographical sketch.

J.22   Milosh, Joseph. "John Gardner's *Grendel*: Sources and
        Analogues." *Contemporary Literature*, 19 (Winter 1978), 48–57.

J.23   Minugh, David. "John Gardner Constructs *Grendel's Uni-
        verse*." *Studies in English Philology, Linguistics, and Literature:
        Presented to Alarik Rynell 7 March 1978*. Ed. Mats Rydén and

Lennart A. Björk. Stockholm Studies in English, 46. Stockholm: Almqvist & Wiksell, 1978, 125–41.

J.24 Morace, Robert A. "John Gardner's *The Sunlight Dialogues*: A Giant (Paperback) Leap Backwards." *Notes on Contemporary Literature*, 8 (September 1978), 5–6. Notes textual error in Ballantine edition.

J.25 Murr, Judy Smith. "John Gardner's Order and Disorder: *Grendel* and *The Sunlight Dialogues*." *Critique*, 18, No. 2 (1976), 97–108.

J.26 Murray, G. E. " The Blue Plate Special." *Fiction International*, Nos. 2–3 (1974), pp. 124–26. Review essay on *Nickel Mountain*, drawing on *The Sunlight Dialogues*.

J.27 Perkins, James Ashbrook. "Robert Coover and John Gardner: What Can We Do with the Poets?" *Notes on Contemporary Literature*, 6 (March 1976), 2–3. Discusses *Grendel*.

J.28 Rudd, Jay. "Gardner's Grendel and *Beowulf*: Humanizing the Monster." *Thoth*, 14 (Spring–Fall 1974), 3–17.

J.29 Shorris, Earl. "In Defense of the Children of Cain." *Harper's Magazine*, 247 (August 1973), 90–92. Review essay on *The Resurrection, The Wreckage of Agathon, Grendel, The Sunlight Dialogues*, and *Jason and Medeia*; see *CLC*, III, 184–85.

J.30 Stall, Marilyn Hubbart. "Structural Techniques in *Grendel*." *South Central Bulletin*, 38 (Fall 1978), 119. Abstract of paper read.

J.31 Stevick, Philip. "Other People: Social Texture in the Post-War Novel." *Missouri Review*, 1 (Spring 1978), 70–78. Discusses *Nickel Mountain*, pp. 76–78.

J.32 Strehle, Susan. "John Gardner's Novels: Affirmation and the Alien." *Critique*, 18, No. 2 (1976), 86–96. Review essay on *The Resurrection, Nickel Mountain, The Sunlight Dialogues, The Wreckage of Agathon*, and *Grendel*.

J.33 Stromme, Craig J. "The Twelve Chapters of *Grendel*." *Critique*, 20, No. 1 (1978), 83–92.

J.34 ———. "Barth, Gardner, Coover, and Myth." *DAI*, 39 (1978), 876A (State University of New York at Albany).

J.35 Tanner, Tony. "The Agent of Love and Ruin." *Saturday Review*, 1 (6 January 1973), 78–80. Review essay on *The Sunlight Dialogues*, drawing on *Grendel*; see *CLC*, II, 152.

J.36 "The Writer's Lot." *Newsweek Special Issue*, 82 (24 December 1973), 84. Brief biographical sketch.

J.37 Vidal, Gore. "American Plastic: The Matter of Fiction." In his

Matters of Fact and Fiction. New York: Random House, 1976, pp. 99–126. Praises Gardner's imagination and supports his criticism of Barth and Pynchon, pp. 117–19.

J.38   *Who's Who in America.* 40th ed. (1978–79). Vol. I, pp. 1157–58.

K. Reviews of
John Gardner's Works

First publication in magazines and newspapers of reviews of Gardner's works, arranged alphabetically. All reprintings and excerpts in *Contemporary Literary Criticism (CLC)* are noted.

A.III *The Complete Works of the Gawain-Poet*

K.1   Benson, Larry D. *Journal of English and Germanic Philology*, 64 (July 1966), 580–83.
K.2   *Choice*, 3 (June 1966), 306.
K.3   Clark, Cecily. *Medium Aevum*, 36, No. 3 (1967), 285–87.
K.4   Cutler, Edward J. *Library Journal*, 90 (1 October 1965), 4078.
K.5   Garmonsway, G. N. *University of Toronto Quarterly*, 36 (April 1967), 295–301.
K.6   Grigson, Geoffrey. *Country Life* (London), 6 January 1966.
K.7   Howard, Donald. *Speculum*, 42 (January 1967), 149–52.
K.8   Lumiansky, R. M. *New York Times Book Review*, 28 November 1965, p. 28.
K.9   Mehl, Dieter. *Anglia*, 85, No. 1 (1967), 82–90. In German.
K.10   Newstead, Helaine. *Romance Philology*, 22 (February 1969), 358–60.
K.11   *Times* [London], 21 July 1966.
K.12   *Times Literary Supplement*, 21 July 1966, p. 636.
K.13   *Virginia Quarterly Review*, 42 (Winter 1966), xviii–xx.
K.14   Wilson, R. M. *Modern Language Review*, 62 (January 1967), 108–9.

A.IV *The Resurrection*

K.15   *Choice*, 4 (May 1967), 288.
K.16   Halio, Jay L. *Southern Review*, NS 6 (Winter 1970), 250.
K.17   Hicks, Granville. *Saturday Review*, 49 (16 July 1966), 25–26.
K.18   *Kirkus Review*, 34 (1 May 1966), 490.
K.19   Mahoney, John. *Detroit News*, 3 July 1966, Sec. G, p. 3.
K.20   Nelson, Elizabeth. *Library Journal*, 91 (1 June 1966), 2872–73.
K.21. *New York Post*, 18 June 1966.
K.22   *Publishers Weekly*, 205 (4 March 1974), 78.

K.23 Shorris, Earl. *Harper's Magazine,* 247 (August 1973), 90–94.
K.24 S.I.B. *Los Angeles Times Calendar,* 19 June 1966, p. 30.
K.25 West, Paul. *Book Week,* 17 July 1966, p. 12.

A.VII *The Wreckage of Agathon*

K.26 Baldwin, Barry. *Library Journal,* 95 (August 1970), 2716.
K.27 Bannon, Barbara A. *Publishers Weekly,* 98 (13 July 1970), 149.
K.28 *Best Sellers,* 31 (1 March 1972), 547.
K.29 *Booklist,* 67 (1 January 1971), 354.
K.30 Boyd, Robert. *St. Louis Post-Dispatch,* 22 October 1970, Sec. E, p. 3.
K.31 Davis, L. J. *Book World/Washington Post,* 20 September 1970, p. 2.
K.32 Gordon, David J. *Yale Review,* 60 (March 1971), 428–37.
K.33 *Kirkus Review,* 38 (15 July 1970), 761.
K.34 Lehmann-Haupt, Christopher. *New York Times,* 24 September 1970, p. 45.
K.35 Midwood, Barton. *Esquire,* 75 (January 1971), 64, 69–70.
K.36 Pierpont, Phillip E. *Best Sellers,* 30 (1 February 1971), 477–78.
K.37 Shorris, Earl. *Harper's Magazine,* 247 (August 1973), 90–94.
K.38 Wernick, Robert. *Time,* 96 (9 November 1970), 86.
K.39 West, Paul. *New York Times Book Review,* 15 November 1970, pp. 4, 65. See *CLC,* II, 150–51.
K.40 Wolff, Geoffrey. *Newsweek,* 76 (21 September 1970), 101–2.

A.VIII *Grendel*

K.41 Adams, Phoebe-Lou. *Atlantic Monthly,* 228 (October 1971), 135.
K.42 Bateson, F. W. *New York Review of Books,* 30 December 1971, pp. 16–17. See *CLC,* II, 151.
K.43 *Best Sellers,* 32 (1 November 1972), 365.
K.44 *Booklist,* 68 (15 December 1971), 353.
K.45 Boyd, Robert. *St. Louis Post-Dispatch,* 26 September 1971, Sec. C, p. 4.
K.46 Boylan, Mildred. *Rochester* [N.Y.]*Times-Union,* 18 December 1971.
K.47 Brown, Ruth Leslie. *Saturday Review,* 54 (2 October 1971), 48–49.
K.48 Brunt, H. L. Van. *Saturday Review,* 54 (27 November 1971), 46.

K.49 Compton, D. G. *Books and Bookmen*, 17 (September 1972), 83–84. See *CLC*, II, 151.

K.50 Ditsky, John. *Georgia Review*, 26 (Fall 1972), 297–313.

K.51 Foote, Timothy. *Time*, 98 (20 September 1971), 89–90.

K.52 Green, Stephen. *National Observer*, 10 (2 October 1971), 27.

K.53 Harrell, Don. *Houston Chronicle*, 10 October 1971, p. 14

K.54 Howes, Victor. *Christian Science Monitor*, 9 September 1971, p. 13.

K.55 Hunter, Jim. *Listener*, 87 (29 June 1972), 874.

K.56 *Kirkus Review*, 39 (15 July 1971), 762.

K.57 Locke, Richard. *New York Times*, 4 September 1971, p. 19.

K.58 Malm, Harry. *Library Journal*, 97 (15 March 1972), 1180–81.

K.59 Mano, D. Keith. *New York Times Book Review*, 19 September 1971, pp. 6, 12, 14.

K.60 Marsh, Pamela. *Christian Science Monitor*, 26 November 1971, Sec. B, p. 3.

K.61 Maslen, Elizabeth. *Encounter*, 40 (March 1973), 77.

K.62 Monfried, Walter. *Milwaukee Journal*, 11 October 1971, p. 3.

K.63 Murray, Michele. *National Catholic Reporter*, 11 February 1972, p. 16.

K.64 *New Yorker*, 47 (18 September 1971), 142–43.

K.65 *New York Times Book Review*, 5 December 1971, p. 83.

K.66 O'Hara, T. *Best Sellers*, 31 (1 November 1971), 355.

K.67 Prescott, Peter S. *Newsweek*, 78 (13 September 1971), Sec. B, 102.

K.68 ———. *Newsweek*, 78 (27 December 1971), 60–61.

K.69 *Publishers Weekly*, 200 (19 July 1971), 117.

K.70 Sastri, P. S. *Review in American Studies*, No. 6 (June 1974), pp. 89–90.

K.71 Shorris, Earl. *Harper's Magazine*, 247 (August 1973), 90–92.

K.72 *Times Literary Supplement*, 14 July 1972, p. 793.

K.73 *Virginia Quarterly Review*, 48 (Winter 1972), xix.

K.74 Waugh, Auberon. *Spectator*, 229 (1 July 1972), 14.

K.75 Whitmore, Priscilla. *Library Journal*, 96 (1 September 1971), 2670.

A.IX *The Alliterative Morte Arthure*

K.76 Bestul, Thomas H. *Speculum*, 48 (January 1973), 142–46.

K.77 *Choice*, 8 (January 1972), 1451.

K.78 Fry, Donald K. *Library Journal*, 96 (15 December 1971), 4097

K.79 Pierpont, Phillip E. *Best Sellers*, 33 (1 October 1973), 292.
K.80 Robbins, Rossell Hope. *Anglia*, 92, Nos. 1–2 (1974), 231–34. In German.
K.81 Salus, Peter H. *English Studies*, 54 (June 73), 275–76.

A.X *The Sunlight Dialogues*

K.82 Adams, Phoebe-Lou. *Atlantic Monthly*, 231 (January 1973), 100.
K.83 Bannon, Barbara A. *Publishers Weekly*, 202 (9 October 1972), 106.
K.84 Bell, Pearl K. *New Leader*, 55 (25 December 1972), 13–14.
K.85 *Booklist*, 69 (15 February 1973), 549.
K.86 *Book World/Washington Post*, 26 November 1972, p. 15.
K.87 *Book World/Washington Post*, 3 December 1972, p. 5.
K.88 Boyd, Robert. *St. Louis Post-Dispatch*, 24 December 1972, Sec. F, p. 4.
K.89 Brady, Charles A. *Buffalo Daily News*, 16 December 1972, p. 38.
K.90 Bravard, Robert S. *Library Journal*, 97 (1 September 1972), 2751.
K.91 Breslin, John B. *America*, 127 (7 October 1972), 265.
K.92 Burgess, Anthony. *Chicago Tribune*, 17 December 1972, Sec. 9, p. 3.
K.93 Butscher, Edward. *Georgia Review*, 27 (Fall 1973), 393–97. See *CLC*, III, 185.
K.94 Cheuse, Alan. *Nation*, 216 (21 May 1973), 666–68.
K.95 *Choice*, 10 (March 1973), 92.
K.96 Cochrane, Diane G. *American Artist*, 37 (July 1973), 26–31, 65, 70.
K.97 Davenport, Guy. *National Review*, 25 (2 February 1973), 158–59.
K.98 Edwards, Thomas R. *New York Times Book Review*, 10 December 1972, pp. 1, 14. See *CLC*, II, 151–52.
K.99 ———. *New York Times Book Review*, 21 January 1973, p. 30. Edwards explains to a reader that he worked from proof sheets and had not seen John Napper's "remarkable" illustrations.
K.100 Foote, Timothy. *Time*, 101 (1 January 1973), 60–62.
K.101 Fuller, Edmund. *Wall Street Journal*, 6 February 1973, p. 20.
K.102 Hill, William B. *America*, 128 (5 May 1973), 420.

K.103 Holleran, James V. *National Observer*, 12 (27 January 1973), 23.

K.104 Howes, Victor. *Christian Science Monitor*, 20 December 1972, p. 11.

K.105 Kelly, Robert. *Fort Wayne News-Sentinel*, 16 December 1972, Sec. WK, p. 4.

K.106 *Kirkus Review*, 40 (1 October 1972), 1162.

K.107 Knight, Susan. *New Statesmen*, 86 (19 October 1973), 570. See *CLC*, III, 186.

K.108 Lehmann-Haupt, Christopher. *New York Times*, 15 December 1972, p. 45.

K.109 McLellan, Joseph. *Book World/Washington Post*, 16 December 1973, p. 6.

K.110 McNatt, James F. *Southern Review*, NS 11 (July 1975), 716–20.

K.111 Maddocks, Melvin. *Life*, 73 (1 December 1972), 24.

K.112 ———. *Atlantic Monthly*, 231 (March 1973), 98–101. See *CLC*, II, 152–53.

K.113 Murray, Michael. *Commonweal*, 97 (12 January 1973), 332.

K.114 *New Yorker*, 48 (13 January 1973), 92.

K.115 *New York Times Book Review*, 3 December 1972, p. 80.

K.116 Pierpont, Phillip E. *Best Sellers*, 33 (1 June 1973), 104–5.

K.117 *Playboy*, 20 (March 1973), 22.

K.118 Prescott, Peter S. *Newsweek*, 61 (8 January 1973), 62–64.

K.119 Pritchard, William H. *Hudson Review*, 26 (Spring 1973), 233–34.

K.120 *Publishers Weekly*, 204 (22 October 1973), 112.

K.121 Rovit, Earl. *Contemporary Literature*, 15 (Autumn 1974), 549.

K.122 *Saturday Review*, 55 (2 December 1972), 80.

K.123 Shorris, Earl. *Harper's Magazine*, 247 (August 1973), 90–94.

K.124 Sipper, Ralph B. *This World/San Francisco Chronicle*, 7 January 1973, p. 29.

K.125 Sudler, Barbara. *Roundup Magazine/Denver Post*, 24 December 1972, p. 14.

K.126 Tanner, Tony. *Saturday Review of the Arts*, 1 (6 January 1973), 78–80.

K.127 Taylor, Henry. *Masterplots 1973 Annual*. Ed. Frank N. Magill. Englewood Cliffs, N.J.: Salem Press, 1974, pp. 353–56.

K.128 Thompson, Francis. *Tampa Tribune-Times*, 24 December 1972, Sec. C, p. 5.

K.129 Thwaite, Anthony. *Observer* [London], 14 October 1973, p. 38.

K.130 *Times* [London], 18 October 1973, p. 16.

K.131 *Times Literary Supplement*, 23 November 1973, p. 1455.

K.132 Torgerson, Margaret. *Rochester* [N.Y.] *Democrat & Chronicle*, 3 December 1972, *Show*, p. 11.

K.133 *Virginia Quarterly Review*, 49 (Spring 1973), lvi. See CLC, III, 184.

K.134 Wolff, Geoffrey. *Book World/Washington Post*, 24 December 1972, p. 3. See *CLC*, II, 152.

K.135 Wood, Michael. *New York Review of Books*, 19 October 1972, pp. 33–38. See *CLC*, V, 131–32.

A.XI *Jason and Medeia*

K.136 Adams, Phoebe-Lou. *Atlantic*, 232 (September 1973), 118.

K.137 *Booklist*, 70 (1 September 1973), 23.

K.138 *Book World/Washington Post*, 15 July 1973, p. 15.

K. 139 Boyd, Robert. *St. Louis Post-Dispatch*, 1 July 1973, Sec. D, p. 4.

K.140 Bravard, Robert S. *Library Journal*, 98 (15 April 1973), 1307–8.

K.141 Carne-Ross, D. S. *New York Review of Books*, 4 October 1973, pp. 35–36. See *CLC*, III, 185–86.

K.142 *Choice*, 10 (November 1973), 1382.

K.143 Crinklaw, Don. *National Review*, 25 (23 November 1973), 1311–12. See *CLC*, III, 186–87.

K.144 DeFeo, Ronald. *Hudson Review*, 26 (Winter 1973–74), 777.

K.145 Dickstein, Morris. *New York Times Book Review*, 1 July 1973, p. 4. See *CLC*, III, 184.

K.146 *Kirkus Review*, 41 (1 April 1973), 426.

K.147 Kirsch, Robert. *Los Angeles Times*, 18 July 1973, Sec. 4, p. 4.

K.148 *Library Journal*, 98 (1 April 1973), 1198.

K.149 Maddocks, Melvin. *Time*, 102 (16 July 1973), 74.

K.150 Nye, Robert. *Christian Science Monitor*, 18 July 1973, p. 13.

K.151 Pierpont, Phillip E. *Best Sellers*, 33 (1 October 1973), 292–93.

K.152 Prescott, Peter S. *Newsweek*, 81 (25 June 1973), 88–90.

K.153 *Publishers Weekly*, 203 (30 April 1973), 53.

K.154 Shorris, Earl. *Harper's Magazine*, 247 (August 1973), 90–94.

K.155 Thomas, Phil. *New Orleans Times-Picayune*, 19 August 1973, Sec. 3, p. 11.

K.156 Walsh, Chad. *Chicago Tribune*, 1 July 1973, Sec. 7, p. 3.

K.157 Weales, Gerald, *Hudson Review*, 26 (Winter 1973–74), 777. See *CLC*, III, 187.

A.XII *Nickel Mountain*

K.158 Adams, Phoebe-Lou. *Atlantic*, 233 (February 1974), 96.

K.159 *Booklist*, 15 February 1974, p. 632.

K.160 *Book World/Washington Post,* 8 December 1974, p. 8.

K.161 Boyd, Robert. *St. Louis Post-Dispatch,* 23 December 1973, Sec. C, p. 4.

K.162 Boylan, Mildred. *Rochester* [N.Y.] *Times-Union,* 23 February 1974, Sec. D, p. 5.

K.163 Brady, Charles A. *Buffalo Daily News,* 5 January 1974, Sec. A, p. 14.

K.164 Breslin, John B. *America,* 129 (6 October 1973), 250.

K.165 Cheuse, Alan. *Nation,* 218 (15 June 1974), 759–61. See *CLC,* V, 132.

K.166 *Choice,* 11 (April 1974), 258.

K.167 *Christian Century,* 92 (14 May 1975), 502.

K.168 DeFeo, Ronald. *Commonweal,* 99 (1 March 1974), 536. See *CLC,* V, 131.

K.169 Foote, Timothy. *Time,* 102 (31 December 1973), 55–56. See *CLC,* III, 187.

K.170 Fuller, Edmund. *Wall Street Journal,* 30 January 1974, p. 10.

K.171 *Harper's Review,* 27 (Summer 1974), 288.

K.172 Hill, William B. *America,* 130 (4 May 1974), 348.

K.173 Hirsch, Foster. *America,* 130 (27 April 1974), 336–37.

K.174 Howe, Linda. *Rochester* [N.Y.] *Democrat & Chronicle,* 24 February 1974, Sec. H, p. 6.

K.175 Howes, Victor. *Christian Science Monitor,* 30 January 1974, Sec. F, p. 5.

K.176 Jones, A. Wesley. *Masterplots 1974 Annual.* Ed. Frank N. Magill. Englewood Cliffs, N.J.: Salem Press, 1974, pp. 273–77.

K.177 *Kirkus Review,* 41 (1 October 1973), 1122.

K.178 LaSalle, Peter. *National Observer,* 13 (12 January 1974), 21.

K.179 Lehmann-Haupt, Christopher. *New York Times,* 20 December 1973, p. 37.

K.180 Leonard, John. *New York Times Book Review,* 2 December 1973, p. 2.

K.181 ———. *New York Times Book Review,* 2 December 1973, pp. 76–78.

K.182 Lhamon, W. T. *Library Journal,* 98 (1 November 1973), 3283.

K.183 ———. *New Republic,* 169 (15 December 1973), 25–26. See *CLC,* III, 187.

K.184 Lomas, Herbert L. *London Magazine,* 15 (October–November 1975), 105–18. See *CLC,* VII, 115–16.

K.185 Millar, Sylvia. *Times Literary Supplement,* 13 December 1974, p. 1420.

K.186 Murray, G. E. *Fiction International,* 2–3 (1974), 124–26.

K.187 *New Yorker*, 49 (21 January 1974), 94.

K.188 *Observer* [London], 17 November 1974, p. 33.

K.189 *Publishers Weekly*, 204 (1 October 1973), 77–78

K.190 Pumphrey, Martin. *Chicago Tribune*, 16 December 1973, Sec. 7, p. 1.

K.191 *Rochester* [N.Y.] *Times-Union*, 17 October 1973, Sec. B, p. 5.

K.192 Rogers, Michael. *Rolling Stone*, 14 March 1974, p. 75. See *CLC*, III, 188.

K.193 Skow, Jack. *Book World/Washington Post*, 31 March 1974, pp. 1, 4. See *CLC*, V, 132.

K.194 Spacks, Patricia Meyer. *Hudson Review*, 27 (Summer 1974), 282–95.

K.195 Stade, George. *New York Times Book Review*, 9 December 1973, p. 5. See *CLC*, III, 186–87.

K.196 Washburn, Martin. *Village Voice*, 24 January 1974, p. 31. See *CLC*, III, 187–88.

K.197 Wood, Michael. *New York Review of Books*, 21 March 1974, pp. 19–22.

A.XIII *The Construction of the Wakefield Cycle*

K.198 Axton, Richard. *Medium Aevum*, 47, No. 1 (1978), 181–82.

K.199 Blanch, R. J. *Comparative Drama*, 11 (Summer 1977), 177–79.

K.200 Cawley, A. C. *Times Literary Supplement*, 22 November 1974, p. 1324.

K.201 *Choice*, 11 (January 1975), 1630.

K.202 Heinemann, F. J. *Library Journal*, 99 (1 December 1974), 3133.

K.203 Poteet, Daniel R., II. *Journal of English and Germanic Philology*, 74 (October 1975), 572–74.

K.204 Stevens, Martin. *American Scholar*, 44 (Winter 1974–75), 151–56.

A.XIV *The King's Indian*

K.205 Ackroyd, Peter. *Spectator*, 1 November 1975, p. 572.

K.206 Allen, Bruce. *Library Journal*, 99 (15 October 1974), 2619.

K.207 Barnes, Julian. *New Statesman*, 90 (31 October 1975), 550.

K.208 Barras, Leonard. *Sunday Times*, 7 December 1975, p. 41.

K.209 *Booklist*, 71 (15 February 1975), 595.

K.210 Boyd, Robert. *St. Louis Post-Dispatch*, 1 December 1974, Sec. C, p. 4.

K.211 Brady, Charles A. *Buffalo Daily News*, 11 January 1975, Sec. C, p. 8.

K.212 Cherry, Kelly. *Chicago Tribune*, 1 December 1974, Sec. 7, p. 3.

K.213 Cockshutt, Rod. *Raleigh News and Observer*, 2 February 1975.

K.214 Crain, Jane Larkin. *Saturday Review*, 2 (8 March 1975), 25–26. See *CLC*, V, 134.

K.215 DeFeo, Ronald. *National Review*, 27 (28 February 1975), 234–35. See *CLC*, V, 134.

K.216 Derrickson, Howard. *St. Louis Globe-Democrat*, 4–5 January 1975, Sec. D, p. 4.

K.217 Edwards, Thomas R. *New York Review of Books*, 20 February 1975, pp. 34–36. See *CLC*, V, 133–34.

K.218 Fowler, Doreen. *Nashville Tennessean*, 5 January 1975.

K.219 Friedman, Alan. *New York Times Book Review*, 15 December 1974, pp. 1–2. See *CLC*, VII, 112–13.

K.220 Garfitt, *Times Literary Supplement*, 12 December 1975, p. 1477.

K.221 Gelfant, Blanche. *Hudson Review*, 28 (Summer 1975), 309–20.

K.222 Gray, Paul. *Time*, 104 (30 December 1974), 56. See *CLC*, V, 132–33.

K.223 Grumbach, Doris. *New Republic*, 171 (21 December 1974), 24.

K.224 Harris, Michael. *Book World/Washington Post*, 12 January 1975, pp. 1–2. See *CLC*, V, 133.

K.225 Howes, Victor. *Christian Science Monitor*, 19 December 1974, 10.

K.226 Kennedy, William. *New Republic*, 171 (7 December 1974), 19–20. See *CLC*, VII, 111–12.

K.227 *Kirkus Review*, 42 (1 October 1974), 1075.

K.228 Levine, George. *Partisan Review*, 42 (Spring 1975), 291–97. See *CLC*, VII, 113–15.

K.229 Mallalieu, H. B. *Stand*, 17, No. 2 (1976), 74–75. See *CLC*, VII, 116.

K.230 Mella, John. *Showcase/Chicago Sun-Times*, 15 December 1974, Sec. C, p. 1.

K.231 Moody, Minnie Hite. *Columbus Evening Dispatch*, 26 January 1975, Sec. i, p. 6.

K.232 Murray, G. E. *Milwaukee Journal*, 19 January 1975.

K.233 Murray, J. G. *Critic*, 33 (March–April 1975), 71–73.

K.234 Neilson, Keith. *Masterplots 1975 Annual*. Ed. Frank N. Magill. Englewood, N.J.: Salem Press, 1975, pp. 164–66.

K.235 Parrill, William. *Nashville Tennessean*, 12 January 1975, Sec. F, p. 6.

K.236 *Publishers Weekly*, 206 (21 October 1974), 46.

K.237 Smith, R. T. *Charlotte Observer*, 12 January 1975, Sec. B, p. 8.

K.238 *Tampa Tribune-Times*, 26 January 1975, Sec. C, p. 5.

K.239 Thwaite, Anthony. *Observer* [London], 9 November 1975, p. 27.
K.240 Vick, Judy. *Minneapolis Tribune,* 13 April 1975.
K.241 White, Edward M. *Los Angeles Times Calendar,* 2 March 1975, p. 66.

A.XV *The Construction of Christian Poetry in Old English*

K.242 *Choice,* 12 (September 1975), 841.
K.243 Greenfield, Stanley B. *Modern Language Quarterly,* 36 (December 1975), 426–28.
K.244 Hill, Thomas, D. *Anglia,* 95, Nos. 3–4 (1977), 498–500. In German.
K.245 Hunter, Johanna. *English Studies,* 58 (August 1977), 350–53.
K.246 *Library Journal,* 100 (1 November 1975), 2054.
K.247 Parr, Judith Tanis. *Christianity and Literature,* 26 (Fall 1976), 52–53.

A.XVI *Dragon, Dragon and Other Tales*

K.248 Bartley, Edward. *Best Sellers,* 36 (April 1976), 29–30.
K.249 Cole, William. *Saturday Review,* 3 (29 November 1975), 30.
K.250 Elleman, Barbara. *Booklist,* 72 (15 January 1976), 684.
K.251 Horn, A. S. *Horn Book,* 52 (April 1976), 154.
K.252 Ridley, Clifford A. *National Observer,* 14 (27 December 1975), 17.
K.253 Yardley, Jonathan. *New York Times Book Review,* 16 November 1975, p. 29.

A.XVIII *Gudgekin the Thistle Girl and Other Tales*

K.254 Bevington, Helen. *New York Times Book Review,* 14 November 1976, pp. 28, 50.
K.255 Cannella, Mary Laska. *Best Sellers,* 36 (March 1977), 386.
K.256 *Kirkus Review,* 44 (1 October 1976), 1093.
K.257 *Publishers Weekly,* 210 (4 October 1976), 74. Junior Literary Guild selection.
K.258 Ridley, Clifford A. *National Observer,* 15 (25 December 1976), 15.
K.259 *Saturday Review,* 4 (27 November 1976), 34.

A.XIX *October Light*

K.260 Adams, Phoebe-Lou. *Atlantic,* 239 (January 1977), 93.
K.261 Askins, John. *Detroit Free Press,* 9 January 1977, Sec. C, p. 5.

K.262 Bannon, Barbara A. *Publishers Weekly*, 212 (14 November 1977), 64.

K.263 Bedell, Thomas D. *Library Journal*, 102 (1 March 1977), 630.

K.264 *Bookletter*, 6 December 1976, p. 15.

K.265 *Booklist*, 73 (1 November 1976), 391.

K.266 *Choice*, 14 (March 1977), 62.

K.267 Coale, Sam. *Providence* [R.I.] *Journal*, 27 March 1977, Sec. H, p. 16.

K.268 Coppel, Alfred. *This World/San Francisco Chronicle*, 2 January 1977, p. 32.

K.269 DeMers, John. *New Orleans Times-Picayune*, 9 January 1977, Sec. X, p. 10.

K.270 Dickey, Christopher. *Washington Post*, 7 January 1977, Sec. B, p. 10. National Book Critics Circle Award.

K.271 Dickey, Edward. *Best Sellers*, 36 (March 1977), 380.

K.272 Diehl, Digby. *BKS/Los Angeles Times*, 23 January 1977, p. 3. National Book Critics Circle Award.

K.273 Forbes, Cheryl. *Christianity Today*. 21 (18 February 1977), 28.

K.274 Ford, Stephen. *San Francisco Review of Books* (February 1977), 29–30.

K.275 Freemont-Smith, Eliot. *Village Voice*, 17 January 1977, p. 81.

K.276 Fuller, Edmund. *Wall Street Journal*, 20 December 1976, p. 10.

K.277 Halio, Jay. *Southern Review*, NS 13 (Autumn 1977), 837–44.

K.278 Hendin, Josephine. *New Republic*, 176 (5 February 1977), 30–32.

K.279 Hepburn, Neil. *Listener*, 98 (25 August 1977), 254.

K.280 Kendall, Elaine. *BKS/Los Angeles Times*, 19 December 1976, pp. 1, 12.

K.281 *Kirkus Review*, 44 (1 October 1976), 1110.

K.282 Leavis, L. R., and S. M. Blom. *English Studies*, 59 (October 1978), 448–49.

K.283 Leclair, Thomas. *Commonweal*, 104 (4 February 1977), 89. See *CLC*, VIII, 236.

K.284 Lehmann-Haupt, Christopher. *New York Times*, 1 December 1976, Sec. C, p. 21.

K.285 Logan, William. *Chicago Tribune*, 12 December 1976, Sec. 7, p. 3.

K.286 Long, Fern. *Showtime Magazine/Cleveland Press*, 24 December 1976, p. 20.

K.287 *Louisville Courier-Journal*, 9 January 1977.

K.288 McPherson, William. *Book World/Washington Post*, 2 January 1977, Sec. G, p. 1. See *CLC*, VIII, 234–35.

K.289 Maddocks, Melvin. *Time*, 108 (20 December 1976), 74

K.290 Mannering, Margaret. *Boston Sunday Globe*, 5 December 1976, Books, p. 7.

K.291 Morgan, Edwin. *Times Literary Supplement*, 12 August 1977, p. 977.

K.292 Morton, Kathryn. *Norfolk Virginian-Pilot*, 23 January 1977, Sec. C, p. 6.

K.293 *National Review*, 28 (26 November 1976), 1299.

K.294 *New Yorker*, 52 (14 February 1977), 122.

K.295 *New York Times Book Review*, 2 January 1977, p. 2.

K.296 Nordell, Roderick. *Christian Science Monitor*, 8 December 1976, p. 33.

K.297 Olson, Clarence E. *St. Louis Post-Dispatch*, 26 December 1976, Sec. E, p. 4.

K.298 ———. *St. Louis Post-Dispatch*, 9 January 1977, Sec. F, p. 4. National Book Critics Circle Award.

K.299 Ostermann, Robert. *National Observer*, 16 (29 January 1977), 21.

K.300 Paulin, Tom. *New Statesman*, 94 (22 July 1977), 123.

K.301 Prescott, Peter. *Newsweek*, 88 (29 November 1976), 104.

K.302 Pritchard, William H. *Hudson Review*, 30 (Spring 1977), 147–60.

K.303 Prothro, Laurie. *National Review*, 29 (15 April 1977), 452.

K.304 Ravitz, Abe C. *Cleveland Plain Dealer*, 26 December 1976, Sec. 5, p. 28.

K.305 Ray, Lila. *Literary Half-Yearly*, 19 (January 1978), 172–80.

K.306 Reed, Kit. *New Haven Register*, 2 January 1977, Sec. D, p. 4.

K.307 Rubenstein, Roberta. *Progressive*, 41 (February 1977), 59–60.

K.308 Rush, Michael. *Christian Century*, 94 (18 May 1977), 482.

K.309 Stone, Elizabeth. *Village Voice*, 27 December 1976, p. 70.

K.310 Towers, Robert. *New York Times Book Review*, 26 December 1976, pp. 1, 16. See *CLC*, VIII, 234.

K.311 Van Laan, James R. *Magill's Literary Annual Books of 1976*. Ed. Frank N. Magill. Englewood Cliffs, N.J.: Salem Press, 1977, pp. 580–83.

K.312 *Virginia Quarterly Review*, 53 (Spring 1977), 62.

K.313 Wood, Michael. *New York Review of Books*, 20 January 1977, pp. 59–61. See *CLC*, VIII, 236.

A.XX *The King of the Hummingbirds and Other Tales*

K.314 Morris, Theodore C. *St. Louis Globe-Democrat*, 9–10 April 1977, Sec. A, 12.

K.315 Sheils, Merrill, and Frederick V. Boyd, *Newsweek*, 90 (18 July 1977), 92.

K.316 Viorst, J. *New York Times Book Review*, 17 April 1977, p. 50.

A.XXI *Poetry of Chaucer*

K.317 *Choice*, 14 (July–August 1977), 680–81.

K.318 Christopher, M. *U.S. Catholic*, 42 (August 1977), 50. Reviewed with *The Life*.

K.319 Clemons, Walter. *Newsweek*, 89 (11 April 1977), 99–100. Reviewed with *The Life*.

K.320 Donaldson, E. T. *Yale Review*, 67 (Autumn 1977), 100–106. Reviewed with *The Life*.

K.321 Fry, D. K. *Library Journal*, 102 (15 April 1977), 925.

K.322 Fuller, Edmund. *Wall Street Journal*, 20 April 1977, p. 24. Reviewed with *The Life*.

K.323 Hanning, Robert W. *Georgia Review*, 31 (Fall 1977), 732–35. Reviewed with *The Life*.

K.324 Josipovici, Gabriel. *New York Review of Books*, 28 April 1977, pp. 18–22. Reviewed with *The Life*.

K.325 *Kirkus Review*, 45 (1 February 1977), 28. Reviewed with *The Life*.

K.326 Kirsch, Robert. *BKS/Los Angeles Times* (1 May 1977), 1, 13. Reviewed with *The Life*.

K.327 McVeigh, T. A. *America*, 136 (21 May 1977), 469–70. Reviewed with *The Life*.

K.328 Marvel, Bill. *National Observer*, 16 (16 April 1977), 25. Reviewed with *The Life*.

K.329 Milosh, Joseph E. *Cithara*, 17 (November 1977), 58–60.

K.330 Modert, Jo. *St. Louis Post-Dispatch*, 10 April 1977, Sec. D, p. 4. Reviewed with *The Life*.

K.331 Morrison, Theodore. *Book World/Washington Post*, 27 March 1977, Sec. E, p. 5. Reviewed with *The Life*.

K.332 Mudrick, Marvin. *Hudson Review*, 30 (Autumn 1977), 426. Reviewed with *The Life*.

K.333 Muscatine, Charles. *New York Times Book Review*, 24 April 1977, pp. 13, 38–39. Reviewed with *The Life*.

K.334 *Publishers Weekly*, 211 (31 January 1977), 72. Reviewed with *The Life*.

K.335 Rothschild, Victoria. *Times Literary Supplement*, 13 January 1977, p. 43. Reviewed with *The Life*.

K.336 *Virginia Quarterly Review*, 54 (Winter 1978), 14, 16.

A.XXII *The Life and Times of Chaucer*

K.337 Adams, Phoebe-Lou. *Atlantic,* 239 (May 1977), 101.

K.338 *Baltimore Sun,* 17 April 1977.

K.339 Barnard, Judith. *Panorama/Chicago Daily News,* 2–3 April 1977, p. 7.

K.340 Beam, Alvin. *Cleveland Plain Dealer,* 3 April 1977, Sec. 4, p. 26.

K.341 *Booklist,* 73 (15 March 1977), 1060.

K.342 *Choice,* 14 (February 1978), 1644.

K.343 *Christian Century,* 94 (20 April 1977), 412–13.

K.344 Christopher, M. *U.S. Catholic,* 42 (August 1977), 50. Reviewed with *The Poetry.*

K.345 Clark, Lindley H., Jr. *Wall Street Journal,* 15 December 1977, p. 20.

K.346 Clemons, Walter. *Newsweek,* 89 (11 April 1977), 99–100. Reviewed with *The Poetry.*

K.347 Cowen, Janet M. *Review of English Studies,* 29 (November 1978), 471–72.

K.348 Dolan, Terry. *Hibernia* (10 February 1978), 25.

K.349 Donaldson, E. T. *Yale Review,* 67 (Autumn 1977), 100–106. Reviewed with *The Poetry.*

K.350 Ferris, Sumner. *Speculum,* 52 (October 1977), 970–74.

K.351 Freemont-Smith, Eliot. *Village Voice,* 23 (1 May 1978), 77.

K.352 Fry, Donald K. *Library Journal,* 102 (15 April 1977), 925.

K.353 Fuller, Edmund. *Wall Street Journal* (20 April 1977), 24. Reviewed with *The Poetry.*

K.354 Geylio, Michael. *Grand Rapids Press,* 17 April 1977, Sec. F, p. 2.

K.355 Gohn, Jack Benoit. *Baltimore Sun,* 17 April 1977, Sec. D, p. 5.

K.356 Hanning, Robert W. *Georgia Review,* 31 (Fall 1977), 732–35. Reviewed with *The Poetry.*

K.357 Hitchcock, James. *Critic,* 36 (Fall 1977), 74–76.

K.358 Homer, Frank X. J. *America,* 136 (7 May 1977), 428–29.

K.359 Howes, Victor. *Christian Science Monitor,* 20 April 1977, p. 23.

K.360 Josipovici, Gabriel. *New York Review of Books,* 28 April 1977, pp. 18–22. Reviewed with *The Poetry.*

K.361 *Kirkus Review,* 45 (1 February 1977), 28. Reviewed with *The Poetry.*

K.362 Kirsch, Robert. *BKS/Los Angeles Times,* 1 May 1977, pp. 1, 13. Reviewed with *The Poetry.*

K.363 Laut, Stephen J. *Best Sellers,* 37 (July 1977), 121.

K.364 Lehmann-Haupt, Christopher. *New York Times,* 23 March 1977, Sec. C, p. 29.

K.365 Lenaghan, R. T. *Michigan Quarterly Review*, 17 (Winter 1978), 102–7.

K.366 McVeigh, T. A. *America*, 136 (21 May 1977), 469–70. Reviewed with *The Poetry*.

K.367 Marvel, Bill. *National Observer*, 16 (16 April 1977), p. 25. Reviewed with *The Poetry*.

K.368 Modert, Jo. *St. Louis Post-Dispatch*, 10 April 1977, Sec. D, p. 4. Reviewed with *The Poetry*.

K.369 Morris, Robert K. *St. Louis Globe-Democrat*, 7–9 May 1977, Sec. D, p. 4.

K.370 Morrison, John F. *Philadelphia Evening Bulletin*, 3 April 1977, Sec. 2, p. 4.

K.371 Morrison, Theodore. *Washington Post*, 27 March 1977, Sec. E, p. 5. Reviewed with *The Poetry*.

K.372 Mudrick, Marvin. *Hudson Review*, 30 (Autumn 1977), 426. Reviewed with *The Poetry*.

K.373 Muscatine, Charles. *New York Times Book Review*, 24 April 1977, pp. 13, 38–39. Reviewed with *The Poetry*.

K.374 *New Yorker*, 53 (25 April 1977), 149–50.

K.375 *New York Times Book Review*, 23 April 1978, p. 43.

K.376 *Publishers Weekly*, 211 (31 January 1977), 72. Reviewed with *The Poetry*.

K.377 Quinton, A. *Saturday Review*, 4 (16 April 1977), 46–47.

K.378 Rothschild, Victoria. *Times Literary Supplement*, 13 January 1977, p. 43. Reviewed with *The Poetry*.

K.379 Sachs, Sylvia. *Pittsburgh Press*, 10 April 1977, Sec. G, p. 10.

K.380 Scattergood, V. J. *British Book News* (May 1978), 411.

K.381 Skow, John. *Time*, 109 (16 May 1977), 96-K3.

K.382 *Tablet* (4 February 1978), 108.

K.383 *Virginia Quarterly Review*, 54 (Winter 1978), 14, 16.

K.384 Whitman, Alden. *Book World/Chicago Tribune*, 17 April 1977, Sec. 7, p. 3.

K.385 Wilson, A. N. *New Statesman*, 94 (25 November 1977), 735–37.

A.XXIII *A Child's Bestiary*

K.386 *AB Bookman's Weekly*, 60 (14 November 1977), 2820.

K.387 Bannon, Barbara A. *Publishers Weekly*, 212 (12 September 1977), 132.

K.388 Clemons, Walter. *New York Times Book Review*, 25 December 1977, p. 7.

K.389 Cole, William. *Saturday Review*, 5 (26 November 1977), 40.

K.390 Flowers, A. A. *Horn Book.* 54 (February 1978), 62.

K.391 Geringer, Laura. *School Library Journal,* 24 (October 1977), 111.

K.392 Hearne, Betsy. *Booklist,* 74 (1 December 1977), 612.

K.393 *Kirkus Review,* 45 (1 September 1977), 936.

K.394 Millar, Neil. *Christian Science Monitor,* 3 May 1978, Sec. B, p. 4.

K.395 Milton, Joyce. *Book World/Washington Post,* 13 November 1977, Sec. E, p. 4.

A.XXIV *In the Suicide Mountains*

K.396 Adams, Phoebe-Lou. *Atlantic,* 240 (November 1977), 104.

K.397 Bannon, Barbara A. *Publishers Weekly,* 212 (5 September 1977), 73.

K.398 *Booklist,* 74 (1 September 1977), 22.

K.399 *Bookviews,* 1 (December 1977), 66.

K.400 Clemons, Walter. *New York Times Book Review,* 25 December 1977, p. 7.

K.401 Cosgrave, Mary Silva. *Horn Book,* 54 (April 1978), 194–95.

K.402 Dirda, Michael. *Book World/Washington Post,* 20 November 1977, Sec. E, p. 5.

K.403 Geringer, Laura. *School Library Journal,* 24 (December 1977), 54.

K.404 *Kirkus Review,* 45 (15 August 1977), 868.

K.405 Schaeffer, Susan Fromberg. *Book World/Chicago Tribune,* 16 October 1977, Sec. 7, pp. 1, 4.

K.406 Thomas, Phil. *Southern Illinoisan* [Carbondale], 8 January 1978, p. 31. AP release.

K.407 *Virginia Quarterly Review,* 54 (Spring 1978), 67.

K.408 Wiehe, Janet. *Library Journal,* 102 (August 1977), 1677.

A.XXV. *On Moral Fiction*

K.409 Apple, Max. *Nation,* 226 (22 April 1978), 462–63.

K.410 *Atlantic,* 241 (June 1978), 99.

K.411 Beardsley, Elizabeth Lane. *Journal of Aesthetics and Art Criticism,* 37 (Winter 1978), 226–28.

K.412 *Bookviews,* 1 (May 1978), 60.

K.413 Brotman, Barbara. *Chicago Tribune,* 20 September 1978, Sec. 3, pp. 1–2.

K.414 Buckmaster, Henrietta. *Christian Science Monitor,* 8 May 1978, p. 26.

K.415 Caplan, Brina. *Georgia Review,* 32 (Winter 1978), 935–38.

K.416 *Choice*, 15 (November 1978), 1208.
K.417 Davis, Lennard J. *New York Arts Journal*, No. 10 (1978), pp. 25–26.
K.418 Epstein, Joseph. *Commentary*, 66 (July 1978), 57–60.
K.419 Feld, Ross. *Harper's Magazine*, 257 (October 1978), 89.
K.420 Flower, Dean. *Hudson Review*, 31 (Autumn 1978), 530–35.
K.421 Fuller, Edmund. *Wall Street Journal*, 21 April 1978, p. 17.
K.422 Gow, Haven B. *Christianity and Literature*, 28 (Fall 1978), 54–56.
K.423 Graff, G. *Chronicle of Higher Education*, 16 (8 May 1978), 21.
K.424 Gramm, Kent. *Theology Today*, 35 (January 1979), 515–16.
K.425 Green, Martin. *Commonweal*, 105 (18 August 1978), 535–36.
K.426 Howard, Maureen. *Quest*, 2 (May–June 1978), 71–72.
K.427 Johnson, Diane. *Chicago Tribune*, 30 April 1978, Sec. 7, p. 3.
K.428 Kazin, Alfred. *Esquire*, 89 (9 May 1978), 35–36.
K.429 Kellman, Steven G. *Modern Fiction Studies*, 24 (Winter 1978–79), 650–51.
K.430 Kirsch, Robert, *BKS/Los Angeles Times*, 30 April 1978, pp. 1, 8.
K.431 Lehmann-Haupt, Christopher. *New York Times*, 3 May 1978, Sec. C, p. 21.
K.432 Madrick, J. G. *Business Weekly* (24 July 1978), 11.
K.433 May, John R. *Horizons*, 5 (Fall 1978), 283–85.
K.434 Prescott, Peter S. *Newsweek*, 91 (10 April 1978), 94.
K.435 Rovit, Earl. *Library Journal*, 103 (1 April 1978), 753.
K.436 Sale, Roger. *New York Times Book Review*, 16 April 1978, pp. 10–11.
K.437 Schott, Webster. *Book World/Washington Post*, 23 April 1978, Sec. E, p. 3.
K.438 Schwartz, R. L. *Minnesota Daily* [University of Minnesota], 7 May 1978, pp. 12–13.
K.439 Towers, Robert. *New York Review of Books*, 25 (20 July 1978), 30–32.
K.440 Tucker, Carll. *Saturday Review*, 5 (April 1978), 56.
K.441 Walla, Tom. *Critic*, 37 (1 October 1978), 3–4.
K.442 Wolcott, James. *Village Voice*, 23 (10 April 1978), 52–53.

A.XXIX *Rumpelstiltskin*

K.443 Hari. *Variety*, 24 January 1979, p. 98.
K.444 Jacobson, Robert. *Opera News*, 43 (24 February 1979), 50.
K.445 Schauensee, Max de. *Bulletin* [Philadelphia], 27 December 1978, Sec. B, p. 38.

K.446 Toman, Philip A. *Weekly Post* [Newark], 3 January 1979.

K.447 Webster, Daniel. *Philadelphia Inquirer*, 28 December 1978, Sec. B, p. 5.

K.448 ———. *Opera Canada*, 20 (Spring 1979), 27.

A.XXXI *William Wilson*

K.449 Johnson, Eric W. *Library Journal*, 104 (15 January 1979), 195.

B.18 Afterword to *The Red Napoleon*

K.450 Mullen, R. D. *Science-Fiction Studies*, 4 No. 3 (November 1977), 321.
    Gardner's afterword indicates that he is "evidently wholly unfamiliar with the future-war story and its yellow-peril subtype."

E.6 *Papers on the Art and Age of Geoffrey Chaucer, Papers on Language and Literature*, 3 (Supplement, Summer 1967)

K.451 deVries, F. C. *Neophilologus*, 53 (January 1969), 99–101.

K.452 *Speculum*, 43 (April 1968), 392–93.

Afterword
By John Gardner

It's a pleasing and humbling experience to see this bibliographical profile. God knows how many times I've made lists of my novels, stories, and so on—I don't mean after they were written but in the old days, when I was in college and later, not yet published or confident that I would ever be published. In DePauw University, I remember, I had a journal, one of those double-entry ledgers used by lawyers and such, in which I wrote down all sorts of foolish things (plots for stories, bits of poetry, mournful meditations on what I would later learn to call the human condition), chief among them lists of poems and stories I meant to write or had written and hoped someone would publish. What creative energy I put into those lists!—hunched over the ledger, cross-eyed with concentration, forcing myself to be immensely honest (this story I *would* get published; this other I must cross off, it would never see light. . .). They were, those lists, my proofs to myself that I existed, that I was a wonderful person, not at all what I seemed. Poor sad dreamer, I think, looking back at the boy I was; but not specially sad, not specially anything, just hopeful and full of self-doubt, like everybody, like my mother earnestly counting and recounting her thousands of Christmas cards. "Surely such a vast haul of Christmas cards means *something*," she thinks, half unconsciously, and losing count starts all over. So now, reading John Howell's list of "Separate Publications"—XXXI in all (however many that is)—I feel pleasure and then alarm, rolling my eyes toward the ceiling, asking God, *"Is it enough?"* Quickly I snatch a piece of paper and start a list of the things that, though time is running short, I still have planned.

I have no idea what use a book like John Howell's is, to the general public anyway—or rather, alas, to the scholarly and book-collecting public. Its use to me, needless to say, is that it helps me remember things, sometimes with delight, sometimes with embarrassment, always with surprise. One of the things it brings to mind is the horde of poor crippled beasts not listed here, all the bad poems and stories, novels that didn't work, in some cases things I think did work but somehow got lost—all those poems and murder-filled novels of my childhood, my long disquisition (inspired, as I recall, by some biblical commentary of my grandmother's) on Whether Or Not There Are

143

People On The Moon, the only piece of writing I ever did, I think, that so embarrassed my mother that she allowed it to perish. Or I think of all the writing I did at DePauw—reams of early nineteenth-century poetry, stories for creative writing classes, a book-length study of "satire through the ages," which I lost forever by turning it in to DePauw's most famous English professor (at the time), W. D. Pence; no real loss, to tell the truth—a work of blind ambition, not thought. I read, preparing it, what now seems like hundreds of books (it was no doubt more like six); I do remember clearly that, taking those books out of the library, I was persuaded that someday, after I was famous, scholars would go through the library records and discover what fine, heavy books I'd read. I took out and lugged to my room, for that reason, far more books than I intended to look into.

And I remember with special warmth all the writing I did while at Washington University, which Nellie Patterson, my then mother-in-law, lovingly and laboriously typed for me so I could send my writing out, mostly to the *Saturday Evening Post,* which was not amused. I had a bank job at the time (among other things), printing up checks on an antique machine that hissed and took nips at you, also a job checking deposits to see that they'd gone into the right accounts; and since my work began after everyone else at the bank had left, except for an old black janitor who had a very fine radio and sort of danced while he worked, I was free to rush through my business (God only knows how many deposits went into the wrong accounts) and spend most of my time, there in the bank's back room, writing fiction. Naturally when I got home, at maybe nine or ten at night, everybody pitied me, poor hardworking boy, and let me grab a little writing time. That embarrasses me now, reminds me how much of my life, from childhood upward, I've spent cheating my employers and loved-ones to write fiction. Why did it seem so important? I wonder. Even when I was a child, writing under a tractor parked at the far end of some back lot when I was supposed to be plowing or dragging, and then in graduate school, writing all night, skipping classes to write by day, pretending I was studying, convincing my poor wife that I was worked to the bone by classes and my teaching assistantship— terrible page after terrible page, stories, poems, novels—what madness it seems! Well, that is how I've spent my life. It could have been worse, I suppose. As my friend Lennis Dunlap once said to me, "Cheer up, it could've been heroin."

Nevertheless, it seems to me that this book John Howell has done is a catalogue of my shamelessness and deceit. Part of the reason that

I've always stolen so much writing time is that I write so badly. I could never let it be known that it took me so long to achieve mediocrity. I don't mean to say, with rank false modesty, that I haven't improved. But I can't help thinking with a part of my soul, looking at all these pages by John Howell—what a waste of a human life! (I don't mean John Howell's—though that too may be an interesting point.) I imagine as I write this that what I am saying is quite serious, I was never more earnest in my life; but if I ask myself if I therefore intend to stop this nonsense, the answer is, definitely not! I rise with quick defenses: my books give people pleasure—some people, anyway— as other people's books give pleasure to me; in fact more than pleasure: at my best moments, boundless happiness, at my worst, consolation. The only book of saints' lives I ever read (before I became a medievalist) was a book I ran across as a child, about artists. I remember in particular the legend of Van Gogh, how he sacrificed everything—his ear was a mere trifle—for the bitch goddess all artists serve. I apologize for putting myself in a class with Van Gogh, but I know how he felt, if the legend has any truth in it. Writing a piece of fiction, one steps outside time (in a small way, one does the same when playing softball). It's morning, you work; you look up—not an instant has passed—and it's night. Reading is the same, but even a long and difficult book you can read in a few weeks. Writing a novel, you can escape reality for years. I don't mean to say, as I seem to be saying, that I hate reality; I only mean that, except at rare moments, it doesn't compare.

Reading through John Howell's book I am reminded of one other thing worth mention: that I am a terrible liar and a bundle of confusion—no one should ever believe a word I say. In one interview I say that *Finnegans Wake* is the greatest book of the twentieth century; in another interview a few weeks later I say it's nonsense and fakery. I believe both things absolutely, at the time. I think of Marlowe's idea in "The Heart of Darkness," that telling lies has a smell of mortality in it—meaning, I think, that the man who tells lies steps out of reality, loses contact with the world as it is. No doubt that's true. It also has the smell of "mere sincerity" instead of honesty: the smell, in other words, of sentimentality. There are liars and liars, but the kind of liar I am is the one who, automatically and unconsciously, fits truth to the crowd he's with—with liberals a liberal, with conservatives a conservative, except when, for some reason, he's being perverse, in which case with liberals he tells the lies of conservatives, and vice versa. Such a person should never be allowed out of his room, certainly should never be allowed to give interviews. It's a terrible trait, I'll be the first to admit—though also, of course, it's at the heart of my work as a novelist. I imitate without even knowing I'm doing it. I remember once when I was serving as a judge for the Newstadt Books-Abroad Prize and had been meeting for days with critics and writers from around the world, I began to talk with such a peculiar foreign accent there were people who turned to friends for translation. In fact sometimes, as I remember, I spoke gibberish and claimed it was Welsh. (I'm not Welsh. I just say that. I'm not anything, alas.) (This paragraph too is filled with lies. Dear reader forgive me, I can't help myself!) Anyway, I'm astonished, reading these summaries of interviews, at how often and how deeply I contradict myself. With interviewers who want me to be one of those writers who stare into the abyss, I find metaphors to show my profound familiarity with the abyss. With interviewers who smile and wear nice clean suits, I talk of God and the Republican party. Perhaps it's out of that weakness that I write. When you've revised a story maybe twenty times, you've pretty well gotten the lies out, or at least made them consistent. My friend Bill Gass is said to have said that my weaknesses as a writer are "glibness" and "preachyness." Glibness I accept (though I revise more than he thinks; I'm not as smart as he thinks). But preachyness, no. My characters all preach— they prattle on endlessly, all on different sides—but if Bill Gass thinks I take one side more than another he knows more about my writing than I do. I am all the universe (me and Walt Whitman), confused and untrackable as an electron. I do not deny that when I write I have certain ideas in mind, and a certain, so to speak, moral earnestness; but in the end I let everybody win and lose—no hits, no runs, no errors.

Well, enough by way of an afterword. I thank my longtime friend John Howell for his astonishing kindness, not just in putting this book together but in soft-pedaling my frailties, which he now knows better than anyone else alive, including myself. Even my biography he knows better than I do, accounting for the years I didn't notice as they passed, my mind engaged elsewhere. And I thank in advance those critics and scholars who, armed with this weapon, do not make too much of my weaknesses, specially my disparaging remarks about fellow writers whose works I've read with pleasure and sometimes awe, though at times I forget that, needing some illustration for this or that stupid aesthetic opinion and grabbing out at random, holding up some friend like Donald Barthelme or Bill Gass by a leg or ear and

pointing with momentary idiot scorn at a slightly red eye or missha-
pen toenail. As for anyone else who may read this strange book,
especially anyone young and ambitious, let it be a lesson to you! Be a
farmer or an engineer, don't write! or if you must write, be like
Salinger: *Hide out! Mum's the word!*

Index to Sections A.–I.